Technocratic Politics

This book considers the role of experts and expertise in contemporary politics and the ways in which digitalisation and the use of techniques are transforming practices of governance.

Asking whether the Covid-19 crisis is likely to further advance or weaken these processes, it examines their impact on the future of democracy and urges rejection of the idea of technocracy as an alternative to politics. An examination of the relationship between social élites and technique, this volume highlights the threat posed to representative democracy of this fundamental mechanism of governance in the global world and reflects upon new forms of the political-economic regime.

It is important reading for scholars of sociology and politics with interests in questions of power, governance, and representation.

Francesco Antonelli is Professor of General Sociology in the Department of Political Sciences at the Università degli Studi "Roma Tre", Italy where he coordinates the Bachelor's Degree in "Policies, Cooperation and Development". He is also the Coordinator of the HORIZON2020 Project "PARTICIPATION: Analyzing and Preventing Violent Extremism Via Participation" (2020–2023) and Secretary of the RC "Sociological Theory and Social Transformations" at the Italian Association of Sociology (AIS).

Routledge Studies in Political Sociology

This series presents the latest research in political sociology. It welcomes both theoretical and empirical studies that pay close attention to the dynamics of power, popular protest and social movements, as well as work that engages in debates surrounding globalisation, democracy and political economy.

Titles in this series

Technocratic Politics

Beyond Democratic Society?

Francesco Antonelli

R Routledge
Taylor & Francis Group

LONDON AND NEW YORK

First published 2023
by Routledge
4 Park Square, Milton Park, Abingdon, Oxon OX14 4RN

and by Routledge
605 Third Avenue, New York, NY 10158

Routledge is an imprint of the Taylor & Francis Group, an informa business

British Library Cataloguing-in-Publication Data
A catalogue record for this book is available from the British Library

Library of Congress Cataloging-in-Publication Data
Names: Antonelli, Francesco, author. Title: Technocratic politics:
beyond democratic society?/Francesco Antonelli. Description: New York:
Routledge, 2023. |
Series: Routledge studies in political sociology |
Includes bibliographical references and index. |
Identifiers: LCCN 2022040551 | ISBN 9781032109251 (Hardback) |
ISBN 9781032109268 (Paperback) | ISBN 9781003217725 (eBook)
Subjects: LCSH: Democracy. | Technocracy–Political aspects. |
Technology and state. | Science and state. | Expertise–Political aspects.
Classification: LCC JC423 .A589 2023 | DDC 321.8–dc23/eng/20221025
LC record available at https://lccn.loc.gov/2022040551

ISBN: 978-1-032-10925-1 (hbk)
ISBN: 978-1-032-10926-8 (pbk)
ISBN: 978-1-003-21772-5 (ebk)

DOI: 10.4324/9781003217725

Typeset in Times New Roman
by Deanta Global Publishing Services, Chennai, India

To Silvia,
a Lifelong Companion

Contents

Introduction

The starting point of our analysis is the decision-making dilemma in the public sphere. In general, such a dilemma has implied four classic questions, at least since the time of Aristotle: Who decides? How are decision-makers selected? What is the basis of their power? What is the basis of their social legitimation? If, in traditional society, decision-making was limited to a few issues (e.g., taxation, war, etc.) and was managed by a circumscribed number of people within a society, mainly defined by its stability (the "society of order", according to Alain Touraine's definition [2018]), these conditions would be completely outdated in the modern age. Such issues taken into consideration in public decision-making will greatly increase: there is no area of economic and social life where public institutions are not called on to take a decision. At the same time, democratisation processes have increased the number of parties involved in decision-making within a society defined by an increasing degree of change, so that change is the main characteristic of modernity, the main "resource" of it in order to solve social problems, as well as the main problem to manage: it is not the case that Auguste Comte (1851–1854) considered "order" and "progress" as key concepts for understanding the modern project, as the latter needs the former to be realised, but the order has been continuously and utterly questioned by progress, even if Comte and the Positivism movement believe such a problem can be definitively solved; an ambition shared by many utopians of the nineteenth and twentieth centuries.

In general, the four classic questions about decision-making have fallen into two problematic axes in modernity: the first is the relationship between "what officially appears" when reading, for example, the Constitution, and "what actually happens" in the corridors of power. The second is the relationship between the economy and politics. Both are based on the modern democratic sensibility because the question is: in the interests of people, when considering the complexity of problems and, in particular, the increasing power of the economic élite in modernity, does the power rule or not?

DOI: 10.4324/9781003217725-1

Such a situation puts the decision-making dilemma at the centre of the public stage. There are three perspectives offered by social theory to analyse this dilemma: the theory of the ruling class, the theory of élites and the theory of pluralism. It is not necessary to analyse them in-depth for our discourse, it is enough to consider that all three discuss the idea that most of society actually governs as well as its politicians, and particularly that elected politicians can decide without the involvement of other socio-economic élites. The idea is the same: the more modernisation continues (and globalisation is fully an expression of modernisation) the more democratic politics based on the sovereignty of people weakens. Paradoxically, concerning everything in the form of a liberal democracy structured on free, competitive and periodic elections as well as the rule of law, global democracy is one of the prevalent government systems today and, practically speaking, if the rule of law is actually questioned in a country, every political leader takes into consideration the idea of the "sovereignty of the people", where a single political party represents such a sovereignty (as in China) or an elected, pluralist political class. Formally and symbolically, democracy is strong but more and more people, including intellectuals, think it is getting substantially weaker. Confronting this situation, scholars like Colin Crouch (2000) speak in terms of "post-democracy" to define it, as do others, like Christopher Lasch (1996) who talks about a "revolt of the élites" to underline the increasing distance between people "who decided" in politics, economics and society, and "the other ordinary people". Global capitalism, especially financial global capitalism, seems to be the real holder of public decision-making and, at the same time, neo-populism may be considered to be a reaction to this "lack of real democracy" which, in turn, seems to aggravate problems instead of solving them. Why? Because the idea and the diagnosis are that three levels of power and decision-making exist in the current social system. The first dimension to be considered is at a social level and it concerns people in everyday life facing daily problems. This aspect, defined by authors such as Zygmunt Bauman (2000) as the "politics of life", is also the grassroots for the formation of conflictual collective action and social movement. The second dimension relates to the national polity (Tilly, 1978), and the decision-making space in the public sphere where official and institutionalised actors play their "game of power", facing an audience within legal procedures (constitutions, law, institutions and so on) in a nationally based jurisdiction. This is defined by the democratic process, and it controls the power of the State. For these reasons, it produces legal decisions that are binding for the whole community. The third dimension is constituted by powerful actors in possession of a massive amount of some kind of capital not immediately political (e.g., social capital, symbolic capital, cultural capital and, above all, economic capital), which influences the official decision-making (polity) backstage, outside of both democratic procedures and the citizens' gaze. Within a Marxist framework, this third level has taken root in the economic ruling class, and, for this reason, it is also the venue of a class conflict. This is even more evident, in industrial society: the most significant contribution of scientific socialism has been to address the collective action of the labour movement (and, in general, that of the social opposition to the real power in society) within this fundamental aspect, thus transforming it into a contestable space rather than in a social field managed just by the "establishers".

Reworking this idea, in his leading contribution "The Production of the Society" (1970), Alain Touraine argues that such a "third level" of power must be defined as the "system of historicity" – in other words the space where the society, and particularly modern society, manages itself both reflexively and conflictually, producing a particular kind of change. According to Touraine, the real barycentre of the social system, in an industrial age, is both the size of the conflict between different collective actors rooted in different social classes and the point of integration of these actors/ classes as they share the same values, especially the value of industrialisation, modernisation and so forth – in particular, work and production that were the common grounds on which integration and conflictual dynamics occurred. Nevertheless, this particular balance between conflict and integration, participation and representation, is not a definitive finding. On the contrary, it is just a contingent result: starting with the rise of the post-industrial society, such a balance has become more and more fragile and, in the era of globalisation, it (perhaps) wanes. The "end of Society" (Touraine 2013) is the product of this disintegration: the third level of social power becomes global, self-referential and, above all, is no longer a *permanent* contestable space as it was in industrial society. *Its privileged relationship with a national jurisdiction has been deconstructed* even as the national jurisdiction, in other words, the second level of power; the institutional and official level, continues to exist. Local and global social movements, as well as single protest cycles – e.g., the new global movement at the end of the twentieth century or the Arab Spring and Occupy Wall Street in the early twenty-first century – have challenged the structure of this level, but they have been contingent collective actions. None has taken the place of the working-class movement. The lack of representation and the participation of social actors, particularly from the middle classes and working classes, have become structural facts at global and national/local levels. The system of historicity is ruled by global economic élites who are oriented to the development of the capitalist system. That being said, the lack of permanent contestability of the system of historicity does not mean the absence of a structural stake. When global economic élites are challenged, separately from contingent issues, the fundamental ground of this conflict is the production of subjectivity: a subjectivity that is fully integrated into the system, is functional to capitalist imperatives, is punctually questioned from alternative ideas of freedom, has personal autonomy, maintains "good life" in the community, and has self-expression. According to Alain Touraine (2018), human dignity and rights are often universal values in the name of whichever current social movements occur. At the same time, these collective actions are not always the only way by which the lack of representation and participation manifests itself: as we have already argued above, neo-populism is another way. It is collocated at the level of *national/local* institutions and the official political system. Why? Because this level, even if it is in a post-democratic scenario of emptying, it continues to be both the place of production of binding decisions for the whole community; and a sort of immediate "front office" of the power system for all citizens.

The result of all these processes is that the official political system is between two fires: on one side, the increasing influence of a global and self-referred system of historicity – in other words, global economic élites-while, on the other side, we have the pressure of society, which means the working classes and middle classes can be affected by the consequences of globalisation. Facing a structural crisis of mass democracy rised up at the end of World War II and tied to particular political and social dynamics of the Cold War, the first trend is linked to a model of "formal rights without democratic participation", while the second trend is referred to as a model of "democracy without rights" (in both theory and practice) (Mounk, 2018). In different ways, they express the increasing difficulty of keeping the "rule of law" and "popular sovereignty" together in a global scenario as well as maintaining social development and justice. In recent years, a large number of papers and books have focused on the first part of this problem, defining it as the "neo-populist question" (Anselmi, 2018). Relatively fewer studies have been dedicated to analysing the second aspect, in terms of new governance systems and new models of relationships between power and society, élites and non-élites: we define this set of problems as the *technocratic question. Technique and experts are the main actors through which the system of historicity works – producing socioeconomic transformation via increasing surveillance*; and trying to manage the continuous crisis of legitimation that its decisions produce. Since we said that they are just "the main actors" but not *the only* ones to manage the legitimation crisis and to change society, it is clear that some other elements have to come into play: they are the political élites, in particular the ruling political classes, which involve technique and experts in decision-making, usually seeking an accordance with economic élites. We suggest defining this particular "mix" as *technocratic politics.*

Generally speaking, in both common use and scientific debate, the word technocracy often refers to the "government of experts"; a short definition, clearly linked to questions: who decided? Who rules? The most general expression used in reference to them is "experts" – i.e., a category of people defined on the basis of some kind of technical knowledge, often legally recognised, characterising their "identity". This initial consideration says two fundamental things about them: first, experts are differentiated from lay people because of their expertise. As such, they seem to be a sub-group of intellectuals. However, this is only partially true: not all of them are "intellectuals" in the true meaning, with formal and socially recognised qualifications; on the contrary, since the time of the founding fathers of sociology, the more the division of social labour increases, the more specialisation increases within society and, in the end, everyone is a "technician" for someone else and *vice versa*. The risk of extreme fragmentation and massification, as Ortega Y Gasset (1999) argues, and the possibility of creating some kind of social integration, as believed by Durkheim, rests on such assumptions. In addition, an experts may be a person with relevant practical knowledge or manual competence in some field – for example, a house painter or a mechanic – rather than having a formal educational qualification. At an anthropological level a technician is always a *homo faber*, defined by practical know-how, following a specific methodology to do something in the world, as highlighted in the Italian Renaissance, the age from which this expression comes (Garin, 1988). Such a technician makes and uses tools, whether they be conceptual and/or practical. In the modern age, making and using tools is more and more of an "intellectualised process" that requires a formal, certified education. This means that technocracy is based on the idea that people can become decision-makers if *they know what to do* primarily in the society, in the economic and technological sphere, and this knowledge is useful for making better decisions; however, it is not the case like that of Thorstein Veblen (1914), who, considering the rise of a more complex industrial society in the United States at the beginning of the twentieth century, pointed to engineers as the key figures for the government of such a new kind of society, just because engineers could demonstrate that they could combine practical know-how with formal education, based on modern science, and express a higher degree of rationality. Just as quickly, starting in the 1940s, scholars like James Burnham (1941) or, later, John Kenneth Galbraith (1967) indicated that managers should become the new technocratic ruling classes, characterised precisely by a close union between "knowledge" and "know-how". Their power grew due to the increasing role of public and private bureaucratic structures, and their mixture, in every aspect of social and economic life, led authors like Alvin Gouldner (1979) to define them as a new, rising social class. Recently, in a third phase of change, but in line with this interpretative point of view, the "experts" are mainly defined as educated people who use "regulative science" to take or support public decisions (Eyal 2019), and are indicated as the main technocratic subjects.

Nevertheless, such a point of view stressing the "subjective element" is only one side of the coin: the other, paradoxically less mentioned, refers to the root of the word; technocracy can also mean the "government of technique". Thus, technocracy is certainly a specific apparatus of power distribution, but one must not forget that both this distribution and the work of technocracy are possible, thanks to the centrality of a particular form of knowledge: technique. Finally, there is a third, fundamental element that completes the technocratic discourse: "κράτος" or "κρατέω", in other words "the power of government" and it is at such a level that the short circuit begins. Indeed, in the Western tradition, this suffix is the second part of keywords such as "democracy", "aristocracy", "theocracy" and so forth – namely all political systems. However, this is not the case: first, because technocracy, a word born in the USA during the Great Depression of the 1930s (Segal 2005), carries with it an ideological orientation completely misleading when compared to reality, that of a counter-position to "politics". Instead, it has been thought of as a particular way to organise and reorganise state and society in counter-position to a "discretional" and "imperfect" political system like democracy. Second, in the real history of mankind, technocracy has never been a system of government that has substituted other political systems. At most, it has been a set of different tools of power utilised by a variety of socio-political systems around the world, starting with the rise of Fordist-Keynesian industrial society.

In sum, the phenomenon we are facing is a particular *technique of government based on technique and technicians* presented in varying degrees everywhere in modernity, because modernity and modernisation, at both a political and socioeconomic level, mean a triumph of the technique; a (mostly opaque) part of a more general power configuration rather than a totality. It is just when such a technique of power seems to become prevalent and all too visible that we start to speak of it in terms of "technocracy", as if it were an actual alternative political system threatening democracy in particular. On the contrary, most of the time, experts and technique expand themselves to helping more than substituting a particular kind of power/ governance as well as a particular ruling class. For this reason, it is preferable to leave an ambiguous term such as technocracy, to speak in terms of "technocratic politics", an expression that can show the particular intertwining between different actors and different forms of technique assembling in the contemporary scenario to manage the crisis of legitimacy of public decision-making in a global age and to manage social transformation.

The purpose of this book is to offer a contribution in order to develop a specific theory of technocratic politics, discussing its different relevant aspects. Every chapter revolves around a single keyword: rationality, power, ambivalence, emergency. Technocratic politics is based on a particular model of rationality that keeps together "instrumental rationality" and "substantive rationality", and "means" and "aims", going beyond the classic Weberian distinction between these two kinds of rationality and disproving a vision of modernity as an era of the triumph of the first dimension over the second: this will be the subject of Chapter 1.

Chapter 2 will focus on the particular kind of power and domination developed by the technocratic apparatus of the present day. If, at first, technocratic structures and practices were centred on the government of human experts, nowadays expertise is provided increasingly more through non-human actors, with the rise and spread of artificial intelligence and algorithms as well as digital tools in general. Such a process places at the centre of the public stage a new version of the Sartrian category of the "practico-inert" (Sartre, 1960): domination is increasingly impersonal, post-human, pervasive even, because "State" and "Market" – "public power" exercised by public institutions and "private power" due to private companies – are becoming ever more interconnected in the social fabric and everyday life. Nevertheless, we must not forget that, behind these post-human apparatus, are powerful, human actors. First, because algorithms and other Information and Communication Technologies are programmed and realised by humans with their own bias and prejudices; and second, because the development of such tools are funded by powerful élites in order to promote their interests: more wealth, more power, and so forth. In other words, the political sociology of digital technology shows that it is neither politically nor economically neutral.

Chapter 3 is centred on a particular strategy followed by the "technocracy at work" in the form of technocratic politics – i.e., the construction and exploitation of ambivalence in order to avoid social and political contradictions, meaning the "construction" of a specific strategy for the ruling classes. Since the 1980s, contemporary to the rise of a post-industrial society, the concept of "contradiction" has been side-lined and several scholars, including new left intellectuals, have started to speak of complexity and ambivalence. At the centre of such a change is the problem of the nexus between technoscience and politics. The former, technoscience, has become increasingly important as both a productive force and governance apparatus. Our thesis is that ambivalence can be seen as an assembly principle of technocratic politics, useful for avoiding systematic contradiction in an ambiguous and potentially disruptive socio-political situation.

Chapter 4 explores the relationship between emergency and technocratic governance. It focuses on recent technocratic politics during the first phase of the Covid-19 crisis in Italy (spring 2020). Our main hypothesis is that a new, ambiguous, political, technocratic configuration, next to traditional "enlightened despotism", has formed because of different emerging effects linked to a series of trends and tensions at a macro-social level during the stay-at-home phase.

Each chapter is written in a recursive style: we constantly return to the various theoretical categories, particularly on the idea of "technocracy", with the aim of revealing all their related complexities. At the same time, every chapter can be read independently and not necessarily in order.

1 Rationality

Reassembling Technocratic Theory

By completely recovering the Gramscian concept of hegemony and comparing ourselves with both critical social thought and pro-technocratic theory, the main thesis advocated in this chapter is that the technocratic project aims to build a perfectly rational and rationalised society, not only through the elaboration of a discourse on the means (instrumental rationality and adaptive rationality) but also on the targets (substantial rationality). Even better, the mission of any technocratic project as a device of power appears to be precisely that of creating a close union between these two dimensions. Such a statute of technocracy breaks with that tradition of thought and analysis dating back to Max Weber, according to whom modernity would create hypertrophy of the means to the detriment of the targets, leading to the construction of a world that would become gradually more and more bureaucratised – despite the different forms that bureaucracy can assume and has assumed over time.

Max Weber and the Two Rationalities

The fundamental texts to which we must refer here are those of the very famous lectures given by Max Weber in Munich, at the invitation of the *Freie Studentenschaft* (Free student association) on 7 November 1917 and 28 January 1919: *Science as a Profession* (*Wissenschaft als Beruf*) and *Politics as a Profession* (*Politik als Beruf*). Between these dates, the definitive military defeat of the German Empire and the November Revolution took place which put an end to the Kaiser's Empire. After his discharge in 1915, the prerequisites of these conferences lay not only in the resumption of his strictly scientific activity or in his more decisive and tormented presence in the public and political debate but, above all, in the maturation of a political and theoretical position that would later be the foundation of the Weimar Republic itself: an alliance between the working class and the bourgeoisie; between national values and liberal-democratic tradition born

DOI: 10.4324/9781003217725-2

of the Enlightenment with the aim (which soon proved to be a pure illusion) to make the bourgeoisie independent as a leading force with respect to the Prussian aristocracy in order to definitively modernise Germany. The two conferences expressed, first of all, his attempt to make young German intellectuals, the students, protagonists. They provided him with a passionate and realistic vision of the fundamental science-politics-democracy node necessary to guide the future transformation action of post-war society. In this regard, we must in effect remember how the *Freie Studentenschaft*, starting with its leader Alexander Schwab, author of the influential article "Beruf und Jugend" (1917), stirred in the climate of an anti-bourgeois and anti-modern Romanticism that made its own that criticism to the remodelling of the status of knowledge brought about by the rise of capitalism. From the 1920s to 1930s, this would become one of the particular focal points of the theory and criticism of mass society: no longer about *Kultur*, the modern knowledge, "Polytechnic", "Humboldtian", became technical specialism at the service of *Civilisation*, capital and the promotion of the vulgar mass-man (Ortega y Gasset, 1999). It became a mass to which the young university students of the *Freie Studentenschaft* feared they would be destined to belong once they completed their studies. Weber was opposed to all this: first of all, the foundation of *comprehensive sociology* was understood as a theory of action, legal systems and culture, which – placed, as it were, between psychology and legal dogmatics, and developed in a "rigorously scientific-objective", in contrast to the "amateurish formulations of ingenious philosophers" (in particular the followers of Marx) – had to place itself at the service of historical knowledge and therefore also of present time knowledge and its development trends. Such an empirical science, alien and even antithetical to anti-modern Romanticism, was to promote factual knowledge and self-knowledge. In *The Science as a Vocation,* this conception suggests the idea of a mature specialism, capable of looking at the facts with objectivity and competence, without the influence of political and spiritual values. Science and its teaching are autonomous and must provide indications on the most technically effective means to reach a target, even though they cannot and must not in any way decide on the "clash of the gods": the greater or lesser validity of a certain political ideal, which, as such, belongs to a scientifically *undecidable* sphere. On the fundamental level of training, it follows that when Weber points up the distinction between the role of the university teacher, who speaks to the students as a specialist in a scientific discipline, and the role of the educated citizen, who addresses the general public, his main reference is *What Is Enlightenment* (1784) by Immanuel Kant. As for the latter, even for Weber students and citizens, teachers and political leaders, administration, and politics, they all belong to different institutions for their control mechanisms and for their criteria of rationality. Instrumental rationality, aimed at investigating and identifying the most technically effective means, and substantial rationality, permeated with the strength of values, are correlated but fundamentally autonomous: science cannot say anything about the goodness of the objectives, and politics should not (in a modern world, governed by modern reformism) say anything about the goodness of the means. For Weber, everything is played on the individual will of the specialist in economics, sociology, and law, to approach the truth. The truth is that the means do not in themselves suggest targets: taking it to the extreme, a gun, as such, does not suggest that it be used to kill an innocent person or, on the contrary, to defend a life threatened by a criminal.

In *The Politics as a Vocation* – which, it must be remembered, is a text about the defeat and the tragic impossibility of having political leaders capable of subverting the present – Weber exposes the other side of these ideas, reading them not from the point of view of the Academy but from that of the State. For Weber – as for many of his generation and many others in the twentieth century – politics is always a pedagogical work and a deeply intellectualised relationship with society and between elites: the expert/profane dichotomy completely dominates it, establishing unavoidable hierarchies. In this frame of reference, modern democracy can only be a bureaucratised democracy; carried out in the daily life of society by a body of specialised and technically competent officials (experts), both in relation to the company to be governed and in relation to politicians legitimised by the vote but, often, lacking in experience and "technical" (profane) skills. However, despite its apparent superiority, bureaucracy necessarily needs the "profane", the political guides:

> they represent, for Weber, even the opposite of such officials, as well as of scientists. Just as there are different conception of the scientist and the university teacher, so there are also different conceptions of political leadership. Weber discusses it in the second of the two conferences, drawing the figure of the man who is inspired by a politics of responsibility, in opposition both to one who is inspired by a politics of principles, and to one who is inspired by a politics of power. He must be able to state positions capable of gaining consensus, and must be ready to support them at his own risk. However, he must also come into contact with the "diabolical powers" that are hidden in every use of force, even legitimate ones, and must finally be able to escape their corrupting action. A political guide of this kind deserves to be followed: but it is followed – this is the decisive thing – not by virtue of a "romantic sentiment" or "veneration of power", but by virtue of a rational understanding.
>
> (Schluchter, 2004: 16)

The scientist lives on the determinism emerging from the study of reality and the inescapability of facts; the politician works to break this determinism, and redirect things, while inevitably having to deal with it.

Despite the distinction between scientist and politician, specialist and leader, science and politics, politics and administration, and the exercise of the rationality of means and that of targets, all these areas have a fundamental element in common: being institutionalised in professions. The sense of profession and professionalism is, for Weber, always the same: the almost ascetic exercise of self-limitation as an inner duty to confront the tragic reality without being overwhelmed. The self-limitation of the specialist, who must not be a politician, and of the politician, who must not yield to the "diabolical powers" with which he comes into contact – violence, will to power, material interests. The division of social labour, and the separation of the various spheres of society, structural facts, and "objectives" of modernity, find their subjective precipitate here. The fate of the West recognised by Weber in the rationalisation of society, that is in the progressive domination of the instrumental over substantive rationality, thus also becomes a desirable value; as long as one knows how to stoically and heroically ride it.

A Critique of Rationality in the Name of Rationality

This way of thinking and constructing the modern, of which Weber felt the inevitability but also – as a bourgeois intellectual with a Protestant background – the need for limitation through, once again, a subjective decision, an act of will and responsibility, had an extraordinary influence on the whole history of social thought of the twentieth century. Within an axiological, anti-capitalist, and anti-bourgeois universe, both the neo-Marxist critical thinking on the model and the wake of Critical Theory, and the post-Marxist Foucault-like one, had a strong point in common: understanding the modern – both in its capitalist and socialist version – as the triumph of a subject as the measure of all things; and, therefore, essentially animated by instrumental rationality. In this perspective, instrumental rationality becomes subjective rationality; a way of constructing the living of the modern man in the world and substantially extraneous to any objective, valid, *substantial rationality*, which, on the contrary, characterised the worlds inhabited by the ancients. Correspondingly, the rationalisation process becomes an instrument of domination and discipline in the hands of the holders of power within the society both because it is the dominants who govern this rationality and because it ends up coinciding with that bourgeois utilitarianism typical of the *homo oeconomicus* that, instead of promoting the common good (substantial rationality), denies it in the name of a rationalism that overturns the fundamental Kantian assumption ("treats men not as means but as ends"), reducing every social relationship to a pure "intermediate" instrument.

This is the extraordinary point of convergence of two authors and two very distant methods such as the dialectical one by the Horkheimer of *Eclipse of Reason* (1947) and, twenty years later, the archaeological one used by Foucault in *Les Mots et le Choces* (1966): in the world of classical Greece as in the *Res Publica Christiana* of the Middle Ages, rationality is a *logos* established once and for all and independent of the will of the man; word and speech, ideas and truth are given externally and pervade the world. As taught by Socrates and Plato, rationality must not be built but discovered in every man and every corner of the world. This rationality is objective, coercive, unavoidable, valid in itself. Language reflects the world directly; purposes and meaning prevail over everything and inform the social order. Indeed, they are social facts inscribed in the collective consciousness, we would say with Durkheim, transcendent of the single and that binds them, too; even though in the mythical form of the gods who occupy the place in the Homeric *Iliad* that will gradually begin to fill up subjectivity and its rationality starting from the *Odyssey*. Modernity is thought of as a "fall" and a setting aside of this objective rationality which, even in its maximum expression, the Hegelian one, ends up being subsumed into a senseless and tragic subjective/instrumental rationality. Thus, on the level of powers and institutions, subjective utility asserts itself as the social norm of impersonality and as the value of efficiency and effectiveness, fuelling the growth of those that are thought, according to a mechanistic paradigm of Cartesian memory, as real, new organisational (bureaucracies), productive (assembly lines) and disciplinary (mental hospitals and prisons) mega machines. Tools are useful for every power and whatever purpose because they are insensitive to any power and any purpose. The accumulation of capital is as indefinite as the accumulation of technical means: the power feeds the will to power and *vice versa*, as argued by Mauro Magatti (2009) and everything becomes a mechanism of economic and social development. Instrumental rationality produces the maximum of irrationality and, in its long march, ends up putting an order in itself and rational ordering, as the supreme target-non-target: for the Bauman of *Modernity and the Holocaust* (1989), as well as already for Adorno and Horkheimer in the appendix to the *Dialectic of Enlightenment* (1947) this separation between instrumental (subjective) rationality and substantial (objective) rationality, between the paths of technique and economics and those of emancipation, even if announced and proclaimed from the same common Enlightenment matrix, they are at the basis of the concentration camp epiphany, of the Nazi extermination, of the Gulag. This is a gigantic perverse effect: the emphasis on the means and their accumulation produces, by action or reaction, powerful but hierarchical social institutions, devoid of sense and social responsibility. Therefore, potentially useful also for modern extermination, practically impossible without the technical-bureaucratic means made available by instrumental rationality. The latter thus becomes the essential form of social domination and the stabilisation of the political order: expressing ourselves in Marxian terms and referring to the world before the fall of the Berlin Wall, it is thanks to the progressive triumph of instrumental rationality over substantive rationality that class relations in a given society – favourable to capitalism and the bourgeoisie in the Western world, to the State and party bureaucracy in the world of real Socialism – reproduce and are "secured" from social conflicts. Ending up with radically oppressing individual freedom and desire, within a world that can again become totalitarian (Marcuse, 1974, 1991).

One of the most significant contemporary expressions of recognising this dualism between instrumental rationality and substantial rationality as a constitutive figure of the modern relationship between science, technology and administration on the one hand and politics, democracy and the State on the other, in the name of the triumph of the domination of class, is represented by the *theory of the depoliticisation*; a rather widespread way of approaching both the question of *policy* and *politics* in the face of the emergence of an explicitly technocratic question starting from the 1960s to the 1970s, and especially in the current context of (neo-liberal) globalisation. According to Habermas (1971), the second phase of social rationalisation that began after 1945 placed a new form of bureaucratic domination at the centre of the public scene, in line with what Max Weber had already analysed between 1904 and 1919: the *scientification of politics*. This process would fulfil all the fears expressed by Weber himself in the two conferences mentioned in 1917 and 1919: a complete reversal of roles between the experts and the political class such that the latter would become: "a simple agent of a scientific intelligentsia which, in concrete circumstances, elaborates the implications and objective requirements of the techniques and resources available, as well as optimal control strategies and rules" (Habermas, op. cit.: 63). More than simply overcoming the compromise between bureaucracy and political leadership advocated and theorised by Weber, the modern technocratic form of government requires the expulsion of politics as such from the State, in order to obtain a rational administration of society based on scientific management. The technocratic scientisation of politics, in other words, inevitably means depoliticisation (Habermas, 1971). This depoliticising technocracy would therefore be fundamentally at odds with the practical experiences and involvement of citizens, the influence of interest groups (sic!), the bargaining and the discretion and the leadership of elected representatives. Technocracy would mean that any kind of "social progress can only be achieved by the depoliticisation of problems" (Ridley, 1966, 43). Therefore, instrumental rationality would definitively win over those forms of production and deployment of substantial rationality – which, in Habermas's theory (2017), becomes discursive rationality typical of vital worlds, after the break he made with the centrality of the transcendental subject in favour of the communicative paradigm – opening the way to the colonisation of social life by technology, and to the emptying of democracy. The assumptions are shared by Matthew Flinders and Jim Buller, authors of "Depoliticisation: Principles, Tactics and Tools" (2006), the most influential article on de-politicisation, technique and policies in circulation today. Indeed, according to the two Anglo-Saxon scholars – who never use the term technocracy, placing themselves in the field of public policy analysis – depoliticisation consists of a set of tools and tactics through which the political class delegates to technicians, ad hoc created agencies or specific sets of rules, and entire subjects; in order to create non-conflictual, universal, and politically neutral ways of managing "burning" social problems. Depoliticisation thus understood is, therefore, a particular form of bureaucratic rationalisation which gradually cancels the space of discretion and negotiation typical of political decision. The criticism that this interpretative line brings with it is clear: depoliticisation gradually deletes the spaces of democracy, both representative and direct, helping to create a world that is increasingly administered, impersonal and at the mercy of technology. A world of this kind, therefore, lends itself to being, paradoxically, more and more irrational and inhuman, consuming the meaning and the very basis of social emancipation: this is why the perspective of depoliticisation is adopted with particular enthusiasm by all critics of globalisation, as it seems to reveal in a particularly fitting way the subtle strategies of domination constructed by neo-liberalism – as defined by Marxist geography (Harvey, 1973) and by the perspective on bio-politics (Foucault, 2004).

Technocratic Rationality and Its Advantages

The subsumption of the Weberian thesis on the two rationalities within the universe of social criticism and its re-interpretation as the construction of social domination through the rationalisation/scientisation of public issues is re-proposed exactly reversed in the political and social sense, by the supporters of the technocratic option.

John Kenneth Galbraith, an adviser to President Kennedy and a well-known economist, in his *The New Industrial State* (1967) paper analysed the new mechanisms of government which, in times of consolidated faith in the virtues of Keynesianism and State interventionism, had allowed the extraordinary economic and social growth of the 1950s and 1960s. According to Galbraith, the development of science and technology applied to production had enormously expanded the production possibilities and gave rise to gigantic industrial conglomerates (corporations), which dominated every aspect of individual and collective life. As a matter of fact, it was the society itself that had become a planned and organisational society, that is profoundly shaped by instrumental rationality. From the hands of the business owners (Marx's capitalists), the power, which had become the power to plan, had passed into those of the "technostructure", a variegated group made up of engineers, technicians, administrators, and managers. In this context, the decisive factor was no longer capital, but research. Furthermore, it was no longer consumers who had the power of choice, it was the orientations of the technocrats that determined people's preferences: the classical liberal model (if it ever existed) was gone forever. Faced with the characteristics of the new political economy, the State had assumed a decisive role because, if, on the one hand, it was interested in economic stability and development, on the other hand, large companies could not prosper without public investments in research and development, in university education and the military field both on the "private" and on the "public" side, the system developed multiple synergies based on a growing presence of planning in every institution and sphere of social life. In Galbraith's reading, the personnel employed in the technostructure would thus become a new dominant social subject who, by virtue of a recognised higher education, was able to promote the general interest of society: what was judged by critical theory as the advent of totalitarianism, in Galbraith's enthusiastic reading, became the main vector of social development.

In his *The Coming of Post-Industrial Society* (1973) Daniel Bell discussed the perspectives of technocracy within post-industrial society: the relationship between technostructure and the democratic political order would be the main challenge of the new era. The post-industrial society was characterised by the centrality of scientific knowledge as a factor of development, by the decline of the Taylorist-Fordist factory and by the priority weight of the tertiary sector, both in terms of employees and related to the formation of GDP. In this context, the process of convergence between the various companies of the world continued where, on a national level, growing synergies were developed between the various key institutions of the new production process: the State, the university, foundations, and private companies. The result of all this was the rise of a social space in which the classic separation between "public" and "private" was lost because various subjects would have cooperated, in a not-always-easy way, to achieve the objectives of social and economic development. Although rationalisation and technostructure were increasingly indispensable for both the State and the market, they were faced with the limits of a "politics of passions" and a "politics of interest" which, although largely de-ideologised, continued to play an important role also in post-industrial society. In this context, a great transformation was looming on the horizon that was, at the same time, a great opportunity: technocracy was becoming an agent of modernisation and even democratisation of society itself. In fact, technocracy is based on meritocratic criteria that disregard the old rigidities of social mobility based on income, family origin, ethnicity, or gender. Consequently, the strength of instrumental rationality would have led to a progressive demolition of traditional social and political mechanisms, promoting social emancipation.

A few decades later, this exaltation of the virtues of a social rationalisation, based on the development of techno-bureaucratic structures founded on meritocratic mechanisms of recruitment and management of executive careers, as well as on the role of science and technology as fundamental dimensions of government and social integration, find the basis of contemporary pro-technocratic theories: here, the creation of a neutral public and political space with respect to the Weberian "clash of the gods" – that is, political and ideological values – and all structured by the search for efficiency and effectiveness in as such, asserts itself as the ultimate horizon of governance in the global world. Two of the main exponents of this view are Parag Khanna and Daniel A. Bell[1] who represent, so to speak, the "good cop" and "bad cop" of today's pro-technocratic theory. The point in common between the two scholars is their gaze to the East: for both the new socio-political experiences of reference are the People's Republic of China and Singapore. The two realities that most of all would have adopted the principles of scientific and meritocratic governance of society, based on the exaltation of techno-structures, competent leadership and instrumental rationality as opposed to inefficiency, emptiness, randomness and decisional irrationality of Western representative democracies; first of all the United States, now victims of that degeneration of "public democracy" (Manin, 2017) represented by neo-populism and, therefore, by the presidency of Donald Trump. According to Khanna (2017), indeed, all societies now desire a balance between prosperity and liveability, economic openness and protection, effective governance and listening to the voice of citizens, individualism and cohesion, economic freedom, and welfare. These "do not measure all that on the basis of how 'democratic' the State they live in is, but on how safe they feel in their cities, how much they can afford a stable home and a job, what are their prospects for old age and the chance to keep in touch with their family and friends" (Khanna, 2017: 12). Consequently, planning and statism, market liberalisation and private initiative, can and must co-exist within the structures of the new *Info-State* – that is, the State centred on digital networks, big data, and artificial intelligence and, therefore, deeply interconnected – which the globalisation has shaped. Politics, as well as substantial and axiological rationality (both assumed as a superior form of objectivity and as a place of ideological assertiveness), are completely placed in parentheses by the need for a *good administration*. Pure and simple, without unnecessary ideological discussions but entirely oriented by what is judged to be the best in terms of material results and, therefore, of power politics – both are understood at the collective level and as an "enhancement" of the individual (Magatti, 2009). *Technocracy is the only value in itself*, such as to subsume democracy itself: for Khanna the ideal model of the political-social system is that of a direct technocracy that combines the Swiss institutional model with the Asian one (Singapore and China). That is to say, a technocratic set-up in the formation of the ruling classes and the decision-making process, which nevertheless frequently uses the tools of direct democracy and polls to constantly include citizenship preferences in policy making.

For his part, Daniel A. Bell (2019) focuses mainly on the issue of selecting the political class and on the Chinese model. Although he formulates a diagnosis of the representative democracy practically identical to that of Khanna, he places himself in a more "gentle" way in arguing the desirability of technocracy as a universal model of governance: recognising its limits – in particular, the risk of self-selection of ruling class and therefore of oligarchic degeneration – he underlines how a model of leadership training based not on competitive elections but a system of evaluation, co-optation and enhancement of merit (administrative but also scientific of the officials), is fully sustainable only within the dominant Confucian culture. Given this assumption, Bell traces the same logical steps as Khanna, such as to lead him to recognise how performance, efficiency and effectiveness – all typical values of instrumental rationality – are, in fact, central to judging a political-social system and how each of them is carried out with particular force within a technocratic-meritocratic context such as that of China: from this "instrumentality" a relationship is generated between rulers and ruled entirely as defined by a *substantial democracy* rather than by a formal one:

> An apparent paradox is that Chinese citizens profess faith in democracy while embracing undemocratic government. As Shi Tianjian and Lu Jie observe, however, democracy in the mind of the common Chinese may not correspond to the meaning of the discourse of liberal democracy; it is rather based on *the discourse of protection*. To put it simply, the widely shared opinion is that democracy means government for the people (by the elites), rather than government by the people. Therefore if the Chinese government "serves the people" it is democratic.
>
> (Bell, op. Cit.: 174–175)

Intermediate Considerations

Summarising what has been analysed so far about the role of science, technology, and experts in the articulation of governance, from the point of view of the relationship "instrumental rationality"/"substantial rationality", we can say:

1. Max Weber, from whom this fundamental conceptualisation comes, in the two conferences of 1917 and, above all, of 1919, clearly glimpses how the modern world is characterised by the weakening of the substantial rationality dimension compared to the instrumental one. Corresponding to this is a crisis of political leadership and a strengthening of a highly bureaucratised democracy. On a general level, Weber postulates the incommensurability between the dimension of administrative competence – as well as science – and that of politics, between the identification of the most technically effective means and the establishment of general goals/objectives/targets. Which should correspond, in practice, to a functional separation between the two areas. Finally, the relativisation of science and administrative competence corresponds to a relativisation of the same substantial rationality: it is not the place of definitive truths but that of the clash between different and rival axiological options. Regarding science, the discourse on means and, in general, instrumental rationality cannot and must not say anything. The plans are completely different, even from the theoretical point of view: instrumental rationality as epistemology brings out the "determinism" of the world and the tyranny of facts; substantial rationality is the attempt to break this determinism through beliefs, values, decisions, and wills. Politics is the only place that can and must attempt mediation between these two elements, placing limits on itself as well as on the logical extremisation to which such a dualism leads: for this reason, it is an enterprise characterised by the "tragic", as understood in the tradition of the Greek *polis*.

2. The tradition of critical social thought, faced with a reality recognised as increasingly dominated by social rationalisation and scientification of politics, subsumes Weber's reasoning and relates it – mainly though not exclusively – to Marxism. This entails placing both at the centre of the ideal primacy of substantial rationality over instrumental rationality and understanding the former as a place of absolute rather than relative truths as in the case of Weber: this is why, in a paradoxical way in "progressive" discourse, from critical theory to Foucault, references and comparisons with the classical world abound; the one characterised, precisely, by absolute substantial rationality, the measure

of all things. It ensures a stringent critique of technocratic tendencies, essentially reduced to means of social discipline and of construction of new and more subtle class domination, as well as of the centrality of the transcendental subject – abstraction and glorification of the bourgeois individual – which justifies them on a general theoretical level. Since neither politics nor society, through more radical forms of democracy than the representative one, is conceived as the place where substantial rationality unfolds, depoliticisation is used as an "omnibus category" particularly effective in analysing how instrumental rationality, bent to class purposes, is used, especially in the neo-liberal order, as a process of stabilisation of the system and reduction of the spaces for emancipation.

3. The pro-technocratic social theory, recognising the same "fact" of the extension of the social rationalisation space and the scientification of politics, overturns exactly the order of priority established by critical thinking: primacy is here accorded to instrumental rather than substantive rationality, to depoliticisation *versus* politicisation. From this point of view, Weber's diagnosis of the inevitability of the destiny of reason in the modern world is fully accepted, even though it is "purified" of its tragic sense: the advent and spread of technocracy are good for humanity. The elevation of instrumental rationality to the extent of all things and all governance processes entails the subsumption of substantial rationality and its democratic articulation processes: the relativisation of representative democracy and the instrumental use of forms of direct democracy, both become means for further improving technocratic performance. Even in this line of thought, there is an implicit criticism of the transcendental subject: every technocratic solution, both at the level of selection of the ruling / political class and at that of the elaboration/articulation of policies, entails a certain primacy of the collective on individuals. Therefore, as Gouldner (1970) recognises, for example, utilitarianism rejected on the individual level is, on the contrary, placed at the centre of the socio-political one. The "general will" of Rousseauian memory is put back to the centre and interpreted by the technocrats. Likewise, pro-technocratic theorists are not simply defenders of the *status quo*: on the contrary, they never tire of denouncing the irrationality of the world, and the contemporary Western world, and therefore the need to fully deploy all the potential force contained in the technocratic model.

In all three interpretative lines, it is evident that, independently of the hierarchies built between the two, instrumental rationality and substantial rationality are two dimensions that tend to present themselves as separate and in difficult dialogue with each other. The ideal world hoped for by everybody is the one in which these spheres are perfectly and completely reconciled: the myth of the fall from heaven on earth as well as that of a golden age marked by the fullness of being and rationality dominates the whole discourse on technocracy. The fundamental theoretical and analytical problem is that neither the critical nor the optimistic traditions can see how the very advent of technocracy in the industrial and post-industrial world is already based, in the configuration it assumes, on this reconciliation. This marks a fundamental difference between bureaucracy and bureaucratisation, and technocracy and scientisation that no one seems to want to assume theoretically in all its consequences.

Contributions for a Theoretical Rethinking of Technocracy: Toward the Technocratic Politics

What is technocracy? How can we (re-)define it? It is extremely difficult to answer these questions due to both the variability of the technocratic phenomenon and the many misunderstandings that the term "technocracy" brings with it. First, technocracy has often been confused with the "sophocracy" envisioned by Plato in the *Republic*: a form of a political and social system governed by the wisdom of philosophers and their "ultimate" truths and virtues. On the contrary, technocracy, while bringing with it a certain moralism intrinsic to every kind of social relationship or system of power animated by intellectuals, is a completely modern phenomenon; prepared on the cultural level by the scientific revolution, as well as by the Enlightenment and by Positivism, and, on the material level, by the industrial revolution. Although many of the themes and imaginaries that later merged into the order of technocratic discourse were anticipated in the seventeenth century – especially with Bacon's *New Atlantis* (1627) and the birth of political arithmetic in England (Desrosières, 1993) – it was Condorcet who transformed the revolutionary optimism of the eighteenth century into a real project of the government of society based explicitly on science and technology:

> In *Esquisse d'un tableau historique du progrès de esprit humain*, the famous "testament of the eighteenth century", [...] Outlining the evolution of human progress throughout the course of history, he longs for a capable science to predict the future progress of mankind, to accelerate its pace and guide its course. But, in order to be able to formulate laws that allow us to predict the future, history must cease to be the history of individuals and become the history of the masses; at the same time, it must cease to be a recording of single facts and instead assume

systematic observation as its foundation. Why should the attempt to base the prediction of humanity's future destiny on the results of past history be considered chimerical? "The knowledge of the natural sciences has as its sole foundation the idea that the general laws, known or unknown, that govern the events of the universe, are necessary and constant; and why should this principle be less true for the intellectual and moral faculties of man than for the other phenomena of nature?" Thus the idea of the existence of natural laws of historical development and the collectivistic conception of history were born, in formulations that are certainly still embryonic, but destined to perpetuate themselves, with a continuity that was soon consolidated in tradition, up to the present day.

(Hayek, 1980: 90)

The *Ecole Polytechnique* was established in 1794. Subsequent generations of scientist-philosophers – including Comte and Saint-Simon – had significant and lasting intellectual relationships with it and placed this concept at the basis of their ideas of the modern government of society and economy: political scientism, social engineering, and "planism" were born as fundamental elements of a new technocratic ideology that linked progress to the action of a new elite led by a superior and infallible knowledge. Orientations that, despite what was hoped for in the 1950s by the aforementioned Hayek, not only permeated positivist reformism or scientific socialism but liberalism itself. At the beginning of the twentieth century, this gave rise to orthodox liberalism, whose transformative and regulation of social life has since been extensively analysed by Foucault (2005).

As a fully modern phenomenon, the order of technocratic discourse is therefore entirely based not on the model of the "society of order" (sofocracy) but on that of the "society of change" which subsumes and surpasses the former, as well summarised by the positivist motto "Order and progress". As Alain Touraine (2018) showed, this kind of society elaborates a type of material culture (in the sense that Ferdinand Braudel [1988] gave to this term), of production relations and accumulation dynamics oriented by a radical principle of creativity and innovation. This principle is fundamental: humanity and society build themselves and do so without any idea of transcendence to "produce" and "legitimise" their work. In this context, techno-science – especially the most recent one, focused on digitisation and artificial intelligence – on which every form of technocracy is based, replaces the traditional religions' social sacredness with its own sacredness. Becoming a social governing force through societal change. The image of creativity that guides the process is that of a perfect society in which the effectiveness of the means is consistent with the rationality of the targets. In turn, defined by some kind of philosophy of human nature, to be revealed and realised through technocratic action. For this reason, bureaucracy is another thing compared to technocracy: the first preserves and the second innovates and revolutionises. Bureaucracy means acceptance of Gödel's theorem: to be coherent the system cannot also be complete and seeks its completeness from the outside (politics, substantial rationality). Technocracy lives and develops in the constant attempt to overcome it: it wants to be both coherent and complete, bringing together means and targets.

The second misconception that needs to be dispelled concerns the "nature" of technocracy: technocracy is not and has never been (at least until now) a political and social regime. Technocracy is a social device – that is, a coherent and systematic set of cultures, tools, subjects, institutions, and practices of power – through which, using science, technique and technology, society as a system seeks to improve its ability to intervene on itself. This is why technocracy is not a *hard power* but a *soft power*: it is the prophet initially armed by the hand of a Prince. And it lives *by* and *for* this Prince. In other words, it is genealogically instrumental to the power of a certain social group, party or leader that promotes it. Two main consequences derive from this: technocracy has no masters because it fits well under every master and every master needs it, from fundamentalists to Stalinists, from democrats to turbo-capitalists. The second consequence is that, like every prophet, technocracy ends up building a world of rules, mentality and values which the Prince, at a certain point, in pain of losing his power, can no longer do without technocracy – this does not only mean the government of technicians but, above all, *government of technology*. This ends up producing a more or less rapid, more or less radical change in the composition of the Prince: from Bakunin (1980) who was among the first to reflect on this phenomenon to Burnham (1941) and Gouldner (1979) – just to mention two of the most famous scholars among the many who analysed the phenomenon – the growing role of science and technology and, in general, of scientisation and rationalisation in the world of production as in that of politics and administration, has given rise to a "new class"; a new middle class whose elites form a fundamental part of the ruling class of industrial and post-industrial societies.

Technocracy – a term that spread from the United States of the *New Deal* – therefore has the manifest function of improving the performance of a system with its experts distributed in the various nodes of the political and social power systems; above all, it has the latent function of improving the hegemonic capacity of a dominant social group – of which it becomes, as mentioned, organic – by rewriting the order of discourse and practices. Both in the moments of ordinary administration and, even more, in the emergency ones, also as an alternative to the charismatic and plebiscite solution. Here, hegemony must be understood in the full sense that Antonio Gramsci (2011) attributed to it: not only superior capacity for legitimation and persuasion but also for organisation and production, and more effective problem-solving in an expression of direction. The hegemony of a group is determined when the "words" and the "facts" go hand in hand, achieving higher goals with more efficient means (compared to other social groups). Unity of structure and superstructure, two terms that, not surprisingly, did not appeal to Gramsci, who preferred the more "organic" concept of the social block (Vacca, 2017). Here it is, technocracy always operates as part of a social block and, as we move from early industrial capitalism to organised industrialism and then to the variegated world of post-industrial and global society, as a fundamental part of it: to politics (ephemeral) consensus, to technocracy and technocrats' problem-solving and *decision-making*. More and more automated and post-human with the emergence of artificial intelligence and the dictatorship of the algorithm. In this organic unity of which technocracy is a part, we see the close union between instrumental/adaptive rationality and substantial rationality: technocracy elevates what is pure power and relationship of strength to value; the dictatorship of the party to superior "communist society"; exploitative capitalism in an "open society"; the neo-populist of the Networks as a prophet of the world of deliberative democracy 2.0; political authoritarianism in the fulfilment of Asian values. The institutionalisation of any technocratic discourse and practice is therefore always linked to the promotion of a superior form of society, without which science and technology would make no sense.

This is why it can never be spoken of the neutralisation of politics by technocracy or depoliticisation unless someone would not want to uncritically marry the ideological image that the same technocracy proposes of itself: on the contrary, by recognising the multiple forms in which it institutionalises and develops as well as the tensions it establishes concerning democracy, it is necessary to speak explicitly of "technocratic politics", since within it the political dimension is not at all eclipsed but is exalted according to social and cultural forms deeply inscribed in the traditional phenomenology of power.

Note

1 Daniel A. Bell (1964) is currently the Director of the School of Political Science and Public Administration at Shandong University and a Professor at Tsinghua University and should not be confused with the Daniel Bell (1919-2011) that we talked about previously.

2 Power

Expertise and Digitalisation

After the birth and affirmation of the modern State, one of the most widespread ideas is that, in politics, there is a decision-making centre from which everything starts; that this centre is controlled by the actors who occupy it, through elections, a *coup d'état* or a revolution. The power would therefore have a seat; the outsiders just have to take possession of it or become part of it.

Today, hardly anyone thinks this is still true. For some people, the centres of power within the State continue to exist, but they are no longer politically acquirable: the levers of command have been moved elsewhere, above and beyond the State, now situated in global financial and economic centres. For others, the idea of a decision-making centre is simply obsolete since it refers to a centralistic idea of power and government that is not able to account for the current social and economic complexity. Decision-making centres have multiplied and are scattered at various levels of society, economy, and politics.

Technocracy, as a particular configuration of the knowledge-power-subjects relationship – before the political government – is, in its pure form, a device through which the visible and official centres of power, first of all Parliament, are neutralised in substance: the discretion and autonomy of political and social actors is replaced by the automatism imposed by technology and technical knowledge. The technocratic myth is the myth of the perfect and therefore unique, indisputable, non-negotiable decision. If we wanted to express ourselves in terms of Foucault's analyses, we could say that technocratic politics has more to do with the safety device than with that of discipline, since:

> the safety mechanism tries to cancel the phenomena without resorting to the prohibition [...] but by favoring the progressive cancellation of the phenomena themselves. It is a question of limiting them within acceptable limits, instead of imposing a law on them that says no.
>
> (Foucault, 2003).

DOI: 10.4324/9781003217725-3

If, on the other hand, we wanted to express ourselves in terms of function-alist sociological theory, we would have to say that technocratic politics is part of Luhmann's idea of reducing and organising complexity, rather than Parsons's idea of building a social order understood as a coherent set of moral norms and values. In both cases, power is not conceived as a scarce resource but, above all, as a network of social relations conveyed by the institutions. This happens because, now, there is no longer a clear difference between society and politics, public and market power, or public and private structures. Public institutions and the State depend on private services to function; private services depend on the action of the State and public institutions to exist.

Within this chapter, starting from this interpretative perspective, we therefore question how technocracy works as a system and relationship of power.

Sully or the Relationship between Experts and Machines

Sully is a 2016 film co-produced and directed by Clint Eastwood and star-ring Tom Hanks, which narrates the landing of US Airways Flight 1549 on 15 January 2009 in the Hudson River. The film is based on the autobiog-raphy by pilot Chesley Sullenberger: *Highest Duty: My Search for What Really Matters*. Commander Chesley "Sully" Sullenberger is the pilot of a plane that takes off on the morning of 15 January 2009 from New York's LaGuardia Airport and collides with a flock of birds a few moments later, thus losing the use of both engines. The commander realises that the only way to save all the people on board (his crew and 155 passengers) is to attempt to ditch into the Hudson River; he succeeds the feat without causing any casualties. For this act of immense skill and heroism, Sully is acclaimed and considered to be a hero by the general public; however, he is placed under investigation by the aeronautical body for not following the flight protocol and for putting the crew and passengers in grave danger; even the insurance company accuses him of having caused the destruction of the plane. Torn between feelings of guilt about the damage to the plane and sat-isfaction for having saved a lot of people, Sully must face the Commission of Inquiry who try to prove that, in their professional judgement, he (the pilot) would have had the possibility of landing in airports near the area of the fault. In particular, the prosecution makes use of both computer and flight simulator sessions that refute the thesis that the pilot had no choice but to ditch into the Hudson River. In the film, in a dramatic final sequence, Sully demonstrates that the conditions on which the simulations were based were imprecise and incorrect, as well as offering the privilege of being able to be studied and elaborated over a long-time frame, when, in reality, a pilot who is about to risk an accident has very little time in which to make his decision; Sully made his only (albeit risky) choice, in the few moments he had, which, in his professional opinion, was the only way he could have saved the passengers – he was thus exonerated.

Sully's story highlights some key points for our analysis. First, where specialised knowledge used in a concrete situation is involved, the power is first of all the power to decide (decision-making). This power to decide refers to two areas: first, the human one studied by the theory of action which counts on time, place, means, ends, definitions of the situation and chains of interdependence with other actors – Sully and the crew, who have to manage an emergency situation in a short time *versus* the non-human or post-human one explored by theory of actants (Latour, 2005), in which it is the simulators and on-board computers, together with human beings or, even, without them, that enter into relationship with each other to condition decisions. Second, in a highly formalised technocratic system the relationship between experts (i.e., human beings) and the knowledge they possess cannot be managed at their discretion; however, this relationship is always *mediated and therefore addressed* by specific devices: *hegemony, procedures and automation.* They reduce the space of discretion of the experts (the pilot Sully) even more than the non-experts involved in a certain action (the passengers on the flight). Third, technocratic systems which are based on the imagination of the infallibility of science, on the myth of the *one best way* and on that of neutrality with respect to values and interests when, in reality, they are highly contingent, shaped by specific material interests and bearers of discretionary values; in our film, in fact, it is the insurance companies and the interests of the big airline companies that influence or set the safety and emergency standards. That is when Sully demonstrates that things can be done differently and more effectively. Let's analyse each of these aspects in detail.

The Power to Decide: Humans and Non-humans

Power is one of the great arcana in the history of humanity and, before that, of the human species as we know it. For this reason, despite the fact that tons of books and articles have been written dedicated to this theme, power continues to be a symbol and a myth wrapped in an aura of sacredness – in the double sense of the sacred, that is, of what inspires terror but which, at the same time, exerts fascination and attraction. The more power is defined by an ontology and a realistic epistemology (power as it really is, "naked and raw", and not as it should be) as has happened in the West since Machiavelli, the more it takes on the ambiguous contours of mystery. Becoming a sacred fact again. This is why the greatest narration of power ever written is "The Legend of the Grand Inquisitor" contained in Fyodor Dostoevsky's *Brothers Karamazov* (1879).

The Great Inquisitor or Undesirable Freedom

"The Grand Inquisitor" (Dostoevskij, 2003) is an allegorical tale set in Spain at the time of the Holy Inquisition invented by Ivàn Karamàzov who, in the narrative of the novel, exposes it to his brother Aleksej; a "pure" of heart. Fifteen centuries after his death, Christ returns to earth. He is never mentioned by name, but always called indirectly. Despite appearing furtively, mysteriously, he is recognised by everybody and the people acclaim him as the saviour; however, he is immediately imprisoned by order of the Grand Inquisitor, just as he has carried out the miracle of a resurrection of a seven-year-old girl by uttering, throughout the narrative, his only words: "Talitha kumi".[1] The Inquisitor, who is an old man of almost ninety years, in whose eyes "a spark of fire" shines, immediately goes to the prison where Jesus is being held. In the eyes of the Grand Inquisitor, the scandal represented by the figure of Christ would be the freedom to decide as an absolute ethical and spiritual value that he would donate to human beings; affirming, first of all, before a tempting Satan that "a man does not live by bread alone" and, therefore, rejecting glory and false earthly honours in the name of God and free will. But men soon realised the difficulty and uncertainty into which the "condemnation of freedom", Sartre (1996) would later say, plummets them. And so, weak, inept, and hungry they would again barter an unsustainable freedom with submission to an authority capable of feeding and guiding them: "Feed us, because those who promised us the fire of the heavens did not give it to us". The Grand Inquisitor explains to Christ how a strong and terrible authority is necessary, the one represented by him, which satisfies the true needs of the people by demanding obedience to them; they need to be deceived, paradoxically, in the name of Christ. But in this deception, which is the deception of the powerful and the reality of power – a reality cloaked in simulation that in Saramago's *Gospel according to Jesus Christ* (1991) originates from God himself, in turn manipulator of his son, Jesus – lies the true suffering of the Inquisitor:

> But we will say that we obey you and that we govern your name. In this way we are deceiving them again because we are no longer letting you approach us. And it is precisely in this deception that our suffering is lying since we'll have to lie.

By now, for eight centuries, the Inquisitor and those like him have been with Satan, the only one who can help them realise the work of universal happiness, protecting it from the crazy dream of Christianity, as if to say that the truth will *set* us free, but the lie will *make* us free. There are three forces capable of taking away man's freedom and bringing him back to the right path, truly saving him from himself: the miracle, the mystery, and the authority. Power is order; an order maintained by a select few who know the truth and hide it in secret. At the end of the story, the Grand Inquisitor, after receiving a kiss from Christ, lets him go saying: "go, and never come back".

Power is therefore the true foundation of the social order. Apparently through simulation and violence but, in reality, through the limit it places on the freedom and autonomy of the human being. Power is limitation.

The Limit and the Subject

In the modern theory of power, this feature has been seen either as a source of repression that generates psychic and social distress, or as a mechanism that generates models of subjectivity. Among the supporters of the first position, we find Freud, for whom the *Civilization and Its Discontents* (1930) – or rather of industrial society – consists in the negative consequences that the repression of instincts and freedom in favour of authority would have generated in human beings; in short, the situation described and praised by the Grand Inquisitor, and Bauman who, in the *Postmodernity and Its Discontents* (1997), takes into consideration the opposite scenario: the insecurity and uncertainty in which the inhabitants of the post-industrial world live, having chosen personal freedom at the expense of certainties and authority. Among the supporters of the second position, typically, we find Foucault who, in particular in his *History of Sexuality* (1976), argues that the development of industrial civilisation and, above all, of modernity would be based, not on a repression of freedom but on an exaltation of it, guided and directed towards certain forms functional to the maintenance and growth of collective power. Of the two theoretical positions, Foucault's is certainly the most useful for framing the relationship of freedom/power to decide in a technocratic field.

The power, as a power to decide, does not function as pure impairment and as a limit, neither at the individual level (as Lacan recalls when speaking of the Law of the Father) nor at the strictly social level, since it would result in being functionally useless. The power to decide directs freedom and shapes it, shaping subjectivities. It enables us to act by limiting action itself. At the same time, power in itself, in order not to self-destroy and create order, must give itself a form and self-limit. The history of power (Magatti, 2018), as an aspiration to the full realisation of the control and self-control of humanity over itself, can only be resolved in limited and shaped forms of power and authority. Above all, as a result of social conflicts, the affirmation of constitutionalism as a self-limitation of sovereign power is rooted in the victorious opposition of the productive bourgeoisie respect to absolutism and unproductive aristocracy. If, in the history of modernity, this history of power has passed through three moments – that of the power of the sacred for which it is God who embodies the maximum of control and the possibility of domination, of the politics for what it is the sovereign State that is able to achieve anything, and of the technical-economic, according to which it is capital and machines that make everything possible – even that of power has had the same developments. Ultimately, technocracy is that form of decision-making power which, basing itself on the code of technique, leads power to its maximum degree of development. Technocratic power elaborates decisions that are presented as rational, scientific, effective but also unique, unavoidable, infallible. That is, intrinsically limited and limiting. But who does produce these decisions that limit and enable? If technocratic power is a relationship rather than a resource, is proper decision-making conceivable?

Technical Decisions of Humans and Non-humans

Let put from the point of view of the individual rather than that of systems. The theory of social action, as opposed to that of behaviour, is a theory of decision. It is founded on the idea of a reflective actor who, based on certain means and within a certain situation, tries to pursue an objective by entering into a relationship with others. To act is always to act in a space-time context. And acting, rather than behaving automatically, always presupposes an evaluation and therefore a decision. As it is well known, in the contemporary social sciences, acting/deciding in its pure, rational, transparent form (on the neo-classical model of *homo oeconomicus*) is not considered to be a condition that constantly occurs in people's lives, nor it is considered as a clearly separate modality from automatic behaviour. On the contrary, one of the main contributions made by all the various micro-sociological schools (from Schutz's phenomenology to Goffman's dramaturgical perspective to Garfinkell's ethnomethodology, just to mention the "founding fathers"), consists in showing the complexity of all our actions; more or less conditioned by routines or definitions or roles taken for granted. Which push us to act as we act more by inertia than by conscious and thoughtful decision. Moreover, if, from Simon (1947) onwards, the rationality of the social actor is recognised as limited since he cannot consider all the possible alternatives, and Weich's (1995) contributions have shown, instead, how every decision is more oriented to define things and people rather than to its substantial content, on the whole, it emerges as the image of a highly limited, human social actor, apparently able to decide but who, in reality, does not know how to do it. Even when he occupies relevant organisational and/or social positions. In an era like ours, characterised by an apparent growing personalisation of power, the paradox is this: the social actor is very weak, and subjectivity is a condition that we rarely experience throughout our public and private lives. Consequently, the characteristics of the networks, structures, and institutions, in which we are inserted, enable, or bind, the social actor.

Experts always base their professional and social identity on the denial of this intrinsic limitation of the social actor. From Saint-Simon to the American technocratic movement of the 1930s[2] up to the contemporary reflections of Khanna,[3] the technocratic actor (like any kind of intellectual) as a decision-maker is considered and sees himself as aristocratically superior to the non-expert, precisely by virtue of his training and its cultural capital. The power of competence is based on the assumption of diversity and therefore of the superior effectiveness and efficiency of decisions. This is where technocracy flows into Platonic sophocracy: like the philosopher-kings of the *Republic*, experts think of themselves as having personal characteristics that make them wiser and more able to decide than others. Thus, that rational-legal authority that Max Weber opposed to charismatic power and within which the same technocratic power is usually traced, actually rests on a completely charismatic background and aura (Weber, 2019). Knowledge turns into a moral virtue. And, through this way, in *authentic* decision-making power, since only those who are more autonomous and more "judicious" are able to exercise the power that guides and limits the actions of all the others. The ethics of responsibility and that of disinterest – as already shown by Merton in his analysis of the ethos of science (Merton, 1968) – thus find its maximum expression: the decision of the expert is, by definition, responsible because it is aimed at achieving the end, effectively and efficiently, and weighing all the possible negative and positive consequences, without being influenced by anything else. The technocratic discourse is therefore always a *discourse of responsibility because it presents itself as personally disinterested*; aimed at the universal and the general will (Rousseau, 2004). The technocrat with his superior decision-making capacity is thus the first and the last gardener who prunes the defects of humanity, of which Bauman (1991) speaks. He is the organiser and educator recognised by Gramsci (2011) in the figure of the organic manager/ intellectual.

But what does this idea of disinterest, responsibility, superior decision-making capacity, and perfect power really refer to? To the idea of God. If, for Feuerbach (2012), the keystone of religion is anthropology, we can affirm that of technocracy is theology. The technocratic configuration of the power-knowledge-subjects relationship is based on a narrative that divinises the expert and his decisions, attributing to human beings the particular characteristics of God. Science and technology are really powerful for their pragmatism, systematic doubt, provisionality. All functional imperatives eclipsed in technocratic discourse and practice. The technocratic power that decides thus generates growing expectations in the population that are constantly disproved by internal dynamics. But it is precisely this contact, this longing for the divine disproved by a "human, all too human" technocrat that opens the way to the progressive replacement of the human, technical, decision-maker with the non-human, technical, decision-maker. The history of technocratic power thus becomes the history of a transition to the machine and artificial intelligence, well beyond what Lyotard reported in 1979 in his book, *The Postmodern Condition*. And to their divinisation that marks the contiguity between the human power of the experts and the non-human power of the expert machines – an extremely evident fact in the 1990s of the twentieth century, in the moment of maximum strength of techno-enthusiasm in the face of the rise of the Internet. Intelligent men and machines, working together, would multiply intelligence, knowledge, decision-making abilities, giving life to what Pierre Lévy defined, in his 1996 book of the same title, as *collective intelligence*. Collective intelligence is a divine intelligence that only the human species is able to emanate, thanks to the connectivity of the new machines. From a centralised decision-making power – as we knew it in the twentieth century – we move on to a widespread architecture of power, decision, and expert knowledge. Technocratic intelligence transits into society and spreads; it directly governs lives in social institutions and in real time, thanks to smartphones, tablets, and computers. Becoming the new frontier of the divine in the world (immanence), after the one reached by the political and totalitarian religions of the twentieth century.

This close union of the human and the non-human and the tendential replacement of the first by the second creates the maximum dissimulation of power. If a determined technocratic rationality, instrumental and substantial at the same time, expressed by human beings in flesh and blood is always susceptible of direct attribution of responsibility, when it becomes the impersonal and even dehumanised product of an algorithm, it completely takes responsibility away. Here, the technocratic myth of the perfection of decision reaches its maximum effect.

The Reduction of Complexity through Hegemony

In his neo-systemic analysis, Niklas Luhmann (2012) points out that the true function of power in the reduction of complexity is in the upstream selection of alternatives legitimately pursued by social actors and systems. From this point of view, technocratic politics carries out this original function of power in the most effective way. It places technical knowledge as a mechanism above everything: thus, the complexity of the decision is further reduced. This mechanism is based primarily on the separation of the expert from his knowledge. Since technocracy can be traced back to theology, and systematic doubt to the mystique of decision, it is the unpredictability of the human that must be gradually eliminated; even when it's about an expert who, due to his professional identity, should not be influenced by the limitations of the common social actor.

The reduction of the discretion of the expert as well as the profane is based on three mechanisms: *hegemony, coding based on procedures* and *coding based on automation.*

The Hegemony over Experts: Being Authoritative

As is well known, the theoretical category of "hegemony" was made famous by Antonio Gramsci who made it one of the most important points of his reflection in the *Quaderni del carcere*. In a given historical moment, hegemony is the prevalence of a certain type of ideas on politics and society that dominate the common sense of people, particularly the lower classes. Hegemony, produced by organic-intellectuals, is the key to the consensus and long-term legitimacy of a given political-economic system and its ruling classes. Through hegemony, these classes become executives, in the sense that they are able to direct the development of society without continually using coercion. As redefined in the fields of cultural studies (Hall, 1986), subaltern studies and Immanuel Wallerstein's analysis of the world-system, hegemony is a political way of looking at culture (Wallerstein, 2004). In spite of being little used in studies dedicated to the relationship between science and society, the category of hegemony, rather than that of paradigm (Kuhn, 2012) or others developed within the strong programme of sociology of science,[4] is extremely useful for our purposes. In fact, if, with Bourdieu (1984) and his school, we also consider the cultural field, including technical knowledge and those related to the social sciences, as an area of struggle between different groups and people for supremacy, then it is evident how the affirmation of certain kinds of scientific theories is not only related to their truth in factual terms but also/even to the dominance that, at a certain point, is conquered by one group of scientists/intellectuals over another. This is particularly evident in the sub-field of social sciences, on which technocratic politics is based to a large extent and characterised by a close union between "values" and "facts". For a researcher, access to academic positions, scientific recognition, and the possibility to publish in the most important and prestigious journals as well as to receive public and private funding for their studies, is strongly linked to adhering to a certain hegemonic set of theories. From the international affirmation of the university on the Humboldtian model (close union between research and teaching), through the rise of Big Science after World War II (science and academia in search of large funds), up to the development of the current post-academic model (university as an organic part of economic development) (Ziman, 2000), the institutional organisation of the academic world created the structural conditions for the affirmation of this hegemonic logic that rewards conformity. Starting in the 1970s, the development of quantitative classification methods for journals and researchers (impact factor) – such that a greater number of citations would correspond to greater prestige – and then the affirmation of an oligopoly in the international scientific publishing market have further reinforced this process. Thus, when we consider economic science – which constitutes one of the pivotal knowledge of contemporary technocracy – it is easy to notice that a Keynesian hegemony (state interventionism) has been replaced, starting in the 1970s by a Hayekian hegemony (centrality of the auto-regulated market) and not only linked to the greater or lesser effectiveness of one group of theories with respect to another (truth effect), but also to the ability of the new supporters of "free trade" to interpret the interests of rising economic-political groups and to take root in the heart of the most important universities in the world. It follows that if an economist wants to make a career, he or she must not only start from the assumptions of the hegemonic Hayekian theory but must also grapple with that set of problems and issues considered as decisive by the hegemonic system itself. Thus, today, applied economics, referring to as the real economy, is sharply subaltern and minority when compared to the study of monetary and financial dynamics. As demonstrated by the latest book by Emiliano Brancaccio and Giacomo Bracci *Il discorso del potere* (2019), the Nobel Prize laureate in Economics, is himself strongly influenced by all these dynamics. This is quite evident if we take into consideration some others who have been awarded the prize. Among these is Edward Prescott, whose theories endorse the idea that mass unemployment is only the result of a "voluntary" choice of workers; or Eugene Fama, who, in the aftermath of the great recession, came to argue that the financial market cannot be considered as a cause of the crisis but, on the contrary, should be seen as its "victim"; or Angus Deaton, who believes that the inequalities caused by the mechanisms of the free market represent a necessary fuel to favour economic development. Even Paul Krugman, who today is considered a severe critic of liberalism, was also awarded the Nobel Prize thanks to one of his old theories that exempted speculators from any responsibility regarding monetary crises. As Brancaccio and Bracci point out, this does not mean that economics is a completely arbitrary and ideological science, rather, as also happens to the other social sciences and the natural sciences themselves, it contributes to the construction of the discourse of power; it is strongly influenced by its dynamics.

In general, scientific hegemony is a mechanism which, by destroying and producing symbolic capital, which is prestige, contributes significantly to the formation of the status of "expert" at a certain historical moment. Hegemony ends up constituting a filter and a device of mediation between the expert himself and the knowledge of which he is the bearer since the expert does not freely dispose of the exercise of systematic doubt – and therefore of autonomy – nor, in the phase of accreditation of its competences, in that of their practical exercise. Paradoxically, it would seem that the more a discipline belonging to the field of social sciences adheres to scientism (as in the case of contemporary economics), the stronger is the action of this selective logic set in motion by the hegemonic device. Thus, as, for example, Eduardo Dargent shows in *Democracy and Technocracy in Latin America* (2014), not only is the role of "technocrats", in democratic government processes, the stronger, and the quality of a political class is the weaker, their selection and ability to influence real policies, even beyond the will of the representative institutions, is linked to having attended certain universities, as well as having acquired recognition, and is inserted in the heart of a certain hegemonic scientific-cultural system; in the specific case, neo-liberal and monetarist economic thought.

The Hegemony over the Profane: Science and Technology as Myths

The use of science and technology as mechanisms for legitimising the practices of government and power within all social institutions is a widely studied process and is characteristic of all modern societies. As a species and as individuals, our reliance on science and technology to face, organise and solve practically every problem is so radical that it constitutes a by-now structural and irreversible condition of our very existences: the discourse of science is a real, functional substitute for the ancient reliance on God, religion and theology for answers and decision-making. Thus, relying on construction and support for the social order, just as criticism and conflict rely on the same faith in what is scientific. The very existence of risk dynamics as conceptualised by Ulrich Beck (1986) – that is to say, by the spread of a more critical social attitude towards science and technology in the face of the unforeseen and perverse effects that their practical application entails (for example, of asbestos or "mad cow disease") – is actually the demonstration that the scientific discourse is now essential for life itself, at any level. The concept of hegemony applied to this field helps us to see how this centrality of techno-science is not only the result of the spread of irrational beliefs, supported by politics and economics (as the post-modern version of the traditional argument of the "false consciousness" would have it), but also the incremental result of a series of successes in the domain of nature, such as to make scientific results objectively more efficient and effective than other epistemological systems – magic and science are both political-cultural products that have political-cultural effects but, while the first does not work for the purposes of healing, for example, the second does. It is therefore not science in itself, but the construction of mythology and dogmatics, that is, of the idea of infallibility and redemption through science, what, when used instrumentally, transforms a real effect into a myth. It is this mystification that gives us the basic idea of techno-science as a "funnel". A mechanism that implicitly, more than explicitly, reduces the discretion of social action through soft power rather than hard power. Let's take the case of digital technologies and the network today, so central to social dynamics and the construction of a social body widespread technocracy. As is now widely known in literature, the adoption and success of a particular technology is linked to the belief that this is more effective than those that preceded it and allows those who adopt innovation to acquire credibility, especially in a system where market dynamics are central. The institutionalist theory on organisational myths (Westerlund, 1979) has shown how new technology (for example, the computer) is often adopted by businesses, not always on the basis of a real need, but because the pressures of the environment in which that company is inserted push it to adopt innovation in order to gain credibility with competitors and customers, showing itself, for example, to be modern and in step with the times. Likewise, the technical innovation curve that typically follows a logistic trend (horizontal "S"), can also be considered as a curve of the cognitive attitude towards the technique itself. The very fast rate of diffusion of a particular technique in its initial phase is reinforced by the multiplication of narratives which tend to mythologise the effects where, once established, this tends to be evaluated in a more detached way from the original myths. Therefore, in general, a technique-technology is driven as much by material interests and practical effects as by social imaginaries that legitimise it and place it as part of hegemonic systems of power. The same happens with respect to digital technologies.

First, because these technologies have been inserted within the narrative of the revolution, both in a literal and metaphorical sense, revolution, as social change assisted by technologies (Beniger, 1986), is considered a dominant *topos* in those libertarian and democratic movements, especially in the United States, through whose counter-culture we have passed from the digital network of Arpanet (domain of the military) to the development of the Internet (domain of researchers, first users of the new Network

[Antonelli, 2008]) and the expectation of radical and unavoidable change and a process of rupture and social determinism (Mosco, 2004).

Second, because digital technologies have been based on and favour the development of real impact narratives (Green *et al.*, 2002), and myths and promises were initially mobilised and put in place by the counter-culture and then subsumed by the large economic operators of today's technological infrastructure (Formenti, 2008), the myths have worked as a reconstruction of an epic story in the affirmation of digital technologies whose characters (i.e., Steve Jobs of Apple or Elon Musk of Tesla) and effects (i.e., the idea of immediacy) are projected, in a saving way, today, thus giving life to the myth of irresistibility, social progress and the emancipatory revolution (Balbi and Magaudda, 2014; 2018). The promises regarding the diffusion of expectations of salvation of digital technologies are continuously renewed with each new technological leap, so we can envisage a desirable and easily-within-reach future (Joly, 2010; Jasanoff and Kim, 2015).

This is how we have all been literally "enchanted by the Net" (Formenti, 2000). A narrative mechanism which, alongside the practical one due to the redefinition of the social environment operated by digital technologies, is pushing every contemporary social subject to digitise their life "spontaneously" (for example, even with the simple purchase of a smartphone), implicitly accepting to see one's social action conditioned within the constraints and functions established by digitisation itself (how many people who work today, for example, can really manage without e-mail and not "suffer" the technical and social consequences of using this medium?).

The Reduction of Complexity through Coding

Procedures and Automation

By procedure, we mean the organisation of social behaviours in a series of pre-established sequences that *have to* be carried out by a subject to achieve a certain result. The procedure is the typical juridical figure of administrative law and, equally typically, it is a sequencing of the behaviours prescribed to an expert who operates in a formal institution, as well as to a profane who comes into contact with that institution. Since the time of Max Weber, the procedure is recognised as being one of the characteristic elements of that process of rationalisation/bureaucratisation of the world which, when entailing the affirmation of an impersonal power, becomes indispensable for the maintenance of a large-mass society and is, at the same time, the force that locks up the freedom of each person in a relentless "iron cage"; or it is the condition of any Mr. K in the Kafkaesque absurdities of a *Process* with unfathomable reasons or an unattainable bureaucratic *Castle*. Modernity is so rich in such dystopian imaginaries and situations in which, as experts or pro-fanes we have all found ourselves, that it hardly requires further clarification.

In the era of industrial society and the centrality of the nation-State, tech-nocratic power had the invention of new procedures as its main fallout. In addition, the State possessed a quasi-monopoly of the procedure and man-aged it in a predominantly centralised manner. This is why technocracy and bureaucracy have often been confused when, instead it comes to two dif-ferent decision-making modes that operate in an integrated way; bureau-cracy and bureaucratisation are the effect and limit that technocracy puts on itself. Automation is typical of the post-industrial era, and globalisation, which transforms the procedure into an algorithm and spreads it into pro-duction, is the cultural and social process. If the procedures, that were based on offices, papers and codes, tend anyway to reveal the subjectivity of the human behind them, the advent of the machine completely shifts the atten-tion of users, giving the users the impression of an even greater objectivity (impersonality) of things. Indeed, what is an automated algorithm? In the definition given by Wikipedia, an automated algorithm is:

> a procedure that solves a given problem through a finite number of elementary, clear and unambiguous steps, in a reasonable time [...] The algorithm is a fundamental concept of Informatics, first of all because it is the basis of the theoretical notion of computability: a problem is computable when it can be solved using an algorithm. Furthermore, the algorithm is a key concept even in the programming phase of software development: taking a problem to be automated, programming essen-tially constitutes the translation or coding of an algorithm for that prob-lem into a program, written in a certain language, can therefore actually be executed by a computer by representing its processing logic.[5]

In summary, as automated procedures for transforming information from reality into data, which is at the basis of the production of decisions and actions, algorithms are a triple expression of power.

The Power Effects of Algorithms

First, at the level of political anthropology, since they make it technically possible to establish a boundary between the domain of anthropocentrism and that of post-anthropocentrism, scholars such as Latour (2007) or Di Felice (2017) believe that the advent of a society based on algorithms, entails, for everyone, the spread of a new social ecology in which human beings and, ultimately, their imperfections, are no longer central; the very idea of society would decline in favour of an interconnected and poten-tially more equitable and fairer world of humans and non-humans. Why?

Historically, the West has been built and has expanded through the affirmation of the domination of man (also, and above all, understood to be a male, heterosexual, white, Anglo Saxon, Protestant (or WASP) which is the affirmation of the discretionary and symbolic dimension of a power that engulfs – with its dichotomies "civilised/barbarian", "male/female", "nature/culture" etc. – the world. The post-human of algorithms would therefore put all this into parentheses. In reality, the society of algorithms reserves anthropocentrism (= the power to define and dominate) for the elites who finance and economically or politically exploit the automated algorithms and, in part, for the creative classes (elites of contemporary experts) who realise them (Florida, 2003). On the contrary, post-anthropocentrism, far from being the advent of the new reign of freedom, is the affirmation of a world founded on a new paternalism. What is post-human is also post-humanist and, therefore, in its pure form, non-elites and non-creatives/experts are harnessed in the meshes of an even stronger and denser steel cage.

Second, for the very characteristics that algorithms are assumed as a "code", that is: "as programs that regulate the functioning of a wide variety of social mechanisms and practices through an action on data" (Campo *et al.*, 2018), and as a social discourse that supports these same practices, it is the code that, first of all, should be referred to here. Behind the code are hidden multiple mechanisms of dissimulation of power (Noble, 2018; O'Neil, 2016; Gillespie, 2016) that accompany themselves to processes of non-arbitrary conditioning of human action:

> While the presence of the theory and its implications is more evident in the case of a classical, deterministic algorithm, since it turns out to be nothing more than the automation of a manual process – think of a machine that cooks cream cakes – this human phase of theorization and shaping seems to fail in the case of algorithms used to simulate intuitive skills, designed in a data-driven way thanks to information "digested" during the learning phase. In the case of machine learning algorithms, between the moment of writing the code and the final application, there is a phase during which – according to the scientist interpretation – the algorithm would learn "reality" in an "objective" way from a large amount of classified data. However, both the choice of the dataset and the generation of the data itself are the product of culturally and socially situated human actions, which can introduce systematic distortions in the model.
>
> (Airoldi and Gambetta, 2018: 42)

The code therefore starts from previously established assumptions and categories (ontologies, in computer jargon, or axiomatic) and, through data processing, generates effects that are both desired by those who finance and design the algorithmic code and emergent and unexpected, like all social processes. For example, as Katz points out, algorithms and government through "automated numbers" are not only a form of power but are also completely social "actants" (Katz, 2017), in the sense that they make mistakes and create perverse effects, exactly like human beings do.

It is on this level that the third form of power represented by algorithms develops: that of the social effects of government and the new frontier of the statistical-legal categorisation of individuals that is no longer exercised in a centralistic way but through a collaboration between public institutions and private subjects, that strongly conditions social action. The automated algorithmic procedures mainly produce "rankings" and classifications of the people to whom a certain probability of carrying out or not carrying out a given behaviour is associated. In other words, today, automated categorisation serves mainly to make predictions exploiting much larger datasets than in the past and, on this basis, to support or even determine the decisions of public or private collective subjects. In this case, the main problem is given by the fact that algorithms – especially in their form of *machine learning* (machines that learn) – starting from axiomatic principles, tend to reproduce certain world views and equity criteria (*fairness*) and end up supporting often discriminatory decisions: "the theme of algorithmic justice has therefore proved to be central" (Galeotti, 2018: 80). Let's take into consideration some particularly significant cases: Chen, Hannak and Wilson have recently analysed the impact of gender on the selection of candidates for various jobs in twenty USA cities (Chen, Hannak and Wilson, 2018). The results of their study clearly show that women are systematically discriminated against or hired by offering lower wages, for equal jobs, than or in respect to their male colleagues. Another well-known case is that of the COMPAS (Correctional Offender Management Profiling for Alternative Sanctions) algorithm that is widespread in USA courts with the aim of predicting the risk that already convicted individuals will become repeat offenders. Galeotti writes about it:

> In 2016, the ProPublica news website published the article by Angwin, Larson, Mattu, Kirchner, demonstrating that COMPAS was clearly discriminating against black individuals. In particular, the investigation highlighted that this tool has in some cases very low accuracy rates: a high rate of false positives (that is, individuals falsely indicated as at risk of recidivism) in the case of black individuals, and a higher rate of false negatives (individuals falsely indicated as not at risk) among white individuals versus non-whites.
>
> (Galeotti, op. cit.: 83)

These examples may seem far from the European context or, in general, not very suitable for framing the trend lines of the reconstruction of a technocratic power in the world, because of the difference in the rates of development of the various areas of the globe and the great variety of political regimes present in each area. Actually, these are processes that affect practically all citizens of the world, albeit to a different extent, at least for four reasons. First, the level of global interdependence of communication and socio-economic exchanges is so high that the effects of applying a certain machine learning in any given country – especially if it is as central as the United States – has direct and indirect effects in other parts of the world. For example, the selective logics of fairness that we have seen are practically adopted by all the banks in the world in the management of credit to businesses and citizens, on the basis of the very strong interdependence of world finance. Second, the characteristic of algorithms and their insertion within the Network, and being independent from the territory, literally separating the dimension of time from that of space (Giddens, 1991): by just owning a smartphone and having access to one of the giants of the Internet (Amazon, Google, etc.) to find themselves, at least at the commercial level, within a dimension managed through the logic we have analysed. Third, even authoritarian States such as the People's Republic of China, while systematically disabling access to the services and content made available by the American giants of the platform economy, tend to develop their own digital environments managed with the same techniques and based on logics more "categorising" and "invasive": think of the social credit system which, on the basis of the ideas developed since the 1920s by the British engineer, Charles Douglas, and aim to automatically classify all citizens based on the constant detection of their behaviour, and granting, or not, certain social benefits (Netkin, 2018). And, finally, fourth, the European Union, like other States or public entities, has, for many years, been funding research projects, especially in the area of security, aimed at developing machine learning capable of preventing crimes and, above all, terrorist acts on its own territory. In general, therefore, algorithmic proceduralisation increasingly constitutes a mechanism for the construction of a sort of *society of control and prevention* that strongly binds their decisions and actions to the expert actors operating in the various socio-economic fields and the incorporated common people within the digitisation processes.

The way in which technocracy organises knowledge of the world is therefore the keystone to understanding what its participation in power is really based on.

Notes

1 It is an expression in the Aramaic spoken by Jesus in the Gospel of Mark that means "Little girl, rise".
2 On these points, see the first chapter.
3 On Parag Khanna, see the second chapter.
4 The "strong program" in sociology of science, born in the 1970s, tries to explain the origins and development of scientific knowledge through social and cultural factors and, for this reason, proposes to study scientific theories in the same way, as well as the "true" and the "false" ones. It is opposed to the "weak program" whose main exponent, since the 1940s, has been Robert K. Merton, according to whom the object of the sociology of science is, above all, the scientific institutions and the conditions that make their development possible, not scientific knowledge in itself. On the strong program, M cf. Bloor (1991); on the weak program cf. R. Merton (1968).
5 https://it.wikipedia.org/wiki/Algorithim

3 Ambivalence

Governance and Technoscience[1]

Generally speaking, we live in a time when, confronting social contradictory trends, the majority of social scientists define them in terms of social "ambivalence" rather than "systemic contradiction". During the golden age of industrial society, between the 1950s and 1970s, the opposite occurred: very few scholars (e.g., Merton and Barber, 1976) talked about "ambivalence", as this was typically addressed in psychology, not in sociology. In that period, different viewpoints of sociology towards social contradictory trends are well-summarised by the debate between Karl Popper and Theodor W. Adorno during the Congress of the German Society of Sociology in 1961. Dedicated to Max Weber, it was an important step in the second positivist dispute (Keuth, 2015); incidentally, giving lectures on the logic of the social sciences, the first argues that contradiction is just a "logic problem" to solve and it is neither a methodological nor substantial element of social science explanation, while, following a well-established Marxist tradition, Adorno puts contradiction at the core of both sociological method and society dynamics (Adorno *et al.* 1981). No one spoke in terms of ambivalence.

Since the 1980s, this situation has changed. Contemporary to the crisis of Marxism, real socialist societies and the rise of post-industrial society, the concept of "contradiction" has been side-lined and several scholars, including new left intellectuals, have started to speak of complexity and ambivalence. In other words, such concepts, implicitly or explicitly, are two key ideas within post-modernity or late modernity discourse (Antonelli, 2007).

At the centre of such a change is the problem of the nexus between technoscience and politics: in the new age, technoscience has become increasingly important as both a productive force and a governance apparatus. In other words, as Foucault (2004) argued, technoscience is fundamental for power as well as, we believe, counter-power dynamics themselves. Starting from Lyotard's classical analysis, *The Post-modern Condition* (1979), technoscience is also recognised as a powerful "generating machine" of

DOI: 10.4324/9781003217725-4

an increasing complexity within society; a complexity that can deconstruct the *reductio ad unum* as well as the "obsession with order", both typical in modernity (Maffesoli, 2003; Bauman, 1989).

Three questions about such matters are at the core of this chapter. The first is general and preliminary: more precisely, what is the difference between a theory that stresses the category of "contradiction" compared to a perspective centred on "ambivalence"? The second is more specific: in which sense has the nexus between technoscience and politics been conceptualised in terms of ambivalence within current social theory? The third is incisive: are we actually sure that ambivalence, similar to contradiction, is just a sort of "destiny" in the development of a particular kind of system, instead of the result of an active effort as well as a set of social practices in the field created by the nexus between technoscience and politics (technocratic politics)? Obviously, contemporary Science and Technology Studies (STS) have stressed the role of agency in order to understand the failures and successes of a particular scientific discovery or technological device, beyond the simple production of purely scientific criteria. Nevertheless, our thesis is that the issue is not the agency but the use of contradictory trends co-present or co-generated at the crossroads between politics and technoscience: ambivalence can be seen as an assembly principle of technocratic politics, useful for avoiding systematic contradiction in a socio-political situation.

Contradiction and Ambivalence

The concept of "contradiction" is one of the most important in Marx's theory and, in general, in the modern dialectic method. As it is well-known, such a method has been developed by Hegel, the main source, Marx, who, when "putting it back on its feet", argued what constitutes dialectical movement is the coexistence of two contradictory sides, their conflict and their fusion into a new category (Marx and Engels, 2014). Marx's most important application of the category is to the relationship between capitalism, taken as a historical process, and some of its own subprocesses, among them its development of productive forces, the increasingly social character of its production, and the emergence of the proletariat (Marx, 2018). These structural contradictions are between the process and itself. In other words, it is internal, and it generates many new subprocesses, increasing both the complexity of the system in its own historical development, and instability, irrationality, poverty and disorganisation. Whether, according to Max Weber (2019), the main illness of the capitalist system is the increasing hyper-organisation that leads it towards a social world ever more rigid and bureaucratic (the famous thesis of the "iron cage"), in Marx's perspective the problem, but also the opportunity and the resource, in revolutionary terms, is the opposite; the development of productive forces generates an explosion of the system for its own dynamics, clashing with the relations of production. Therefore, simultaneously, the more capitalism becomes "rationalised", the more it becomes irrational. Managing this structural problem is recognised as the most important role performed by the State following the "Great Depression" (1929), according to all neo-Marxist (e.g., Gramsci, 2011) or critical theorists (e.g., Habermas, 1973), most of whom are interested in understanding why revolution has not exploded in the West as well as by liberal intellectuals (e.g., Keynes, 1936), whose purpose is to stabilise the system. According to Streek (2013), public interventionism, the Welfare State and, above all, creating new debt, have been the "key levers" in managing the internal contradiction of capitalism, and they have also generated the model of democratic capitalism in which structural contradictions are simply suspended. Even if all these analyses are important in understanding the concept of "contradiction" in the relevant parts of modern social and political theories, they do not complete the theoretical sense of such a concept, as an essential part of the discourse of modernity. Under this more general framework, it has to be recognised that the idea of "contradiction" refers to a standpoint in the social world based on the refusal of inconsistencies; and, correspondingly, the glorification of the idea of order and coherence as well as trust towards the feasibility of a society based on such values (Bauman, 1989). Marx and Engels, of course, trust this perspective of all people together involved in the myth of Revolution in the "Short Twentieth Century" (Hobsbawm, 1995). Contradiction is the evil; no contradiction is the good, because the first refers to an incomplete world, and a system cannot manage itself. At the same time, sub-contradictory trends and processes which are made up of a structural contradiction are due to a contingent step on the way to a "resolved world", at the end of history, when everyone will be fully recognised within a Hegelian universal homogeneous State (Kojeve, 1980; Fukuyama, 1992). In the end, contradiction is always an "objective" condition and subjects (included social classes) are *acted upon* or, at best, *had to act*, in considering it.

The discourse on "ambivalence" upsets the discourse based on "contradiction". Merton is the precursor of the use of ambivalence in sociology. He believes it to be the product of conflicting norms and counter-norms associated with particular social positions (Merton, 1976; Merton and Barber, 1963). Nevertheless, the discourse of ambivalence, as an alternative to dialectic perspective, rises just when a new sensibility, new "objectives" of sociological analysis, and a new social world appeared on the stage, at the end of the twentieth century. Regarding the first aspect, starting from a critique on the obsession of modernity with "one-dimensionality", the discourse on ambivalence rejects the image of a world and history without contradictory trends, and, by extension, without cultural and personal diversities, as totalitarian (Bauman, 1991). Whereas the social world in a post-industrial era is a place where conflicts and disorder are permanent conditions like they are in psychological life, as well as at an existential level, and thus people must learn to live in such a complex universe. Therefore, in the newly emergent field of the sociology of emotions, the concept has been examined as an affective experience of mixed feelings or «of contradictory emotions towards the same object» (Weigert, 1991: 21). Smelser, in postulating ambivalence as «the simultaneous existence of attraction and repulsion, of love and hate» (1998: 5), has suggested that it can provide a counter-approach to the dominance of intellectual traditions of rational choice theory by enabling us to consider the «nonrational forces in individual, group, and institutional behaviour» (1998: 3). Eventually, Giddens (1991: 139) considers the "journey of modernity" as one, which will inevitably entail «feelings of ontological security and existential anxiety (which) will co-exist in ambivalence», whereas Beck (1994) has argued that as high modernity «abolish[es] its own ordering categories» (1994: 33) then «irreducible ambivalences, the new disorder of risk civilisation, openly appear» (1994: 12).

"Structure" and "agency" have strictly linked themselves to each other within the discourse of ambivalence: ambivalence, as an unsolvable co-presence of contradictory trends, is a normal condition of agency in the post-industrial and post-modern era, in a structural environment based on complexity, ambiguity and multiplicity. Risk and opportunity are two dimensions omnipresent in everyday life: thus, ambivalence is the new face of the "open society" (Popper, 1945) in the contemporary world as well as the dialectic movement from contradictory to non-contradictory society, which was the main expression of the "faith in inevitable progress of mankind", during the industrial era. Likewise, conceptualising contradictory trends in terms of "contradiction" puts radical conflicts and revolution (the "big crush") at the centre of the history of emancipation; thinking in terms of ambivalence drives towards managing conflicts and a reformist perspective: the mission of social sciences is to highlight ambivalence in social and personal awareness in order to facilitate the adaption of oneself, as well as social institutions (and in particular political institutions), to contradictory phenomena.

In this context, nowadays, the relationship between technoscience and politics is one of the most important fields where ambivalence is growing. Considering the leading contributions of Ulrich Beck and Bruno Latour helps us to understand in which way current social theory analyses and conceptualises ambivalence.

Technoscience in Contemporary Social Theory: The Leading Contributions of Ulrich Beck and Bruno Latour

Although both provide a counterbalance to the postmodernist paradigm through their "constructivist" analyses, Ulrich Beck offers a standpoint based on a humanist, anthropocentric perspective which considers the contemporary age as a phase of radicalisation of modernity (Beck, 1986), while Bruno Latour (1991) works from a post-humanist and anti-anthropocentric standpoint in which the project of modernity, or its "constitution", is opposed to the practical creations of modern society, starting at the beginning of the modern era. What makes Beck's analyses interesting for us and representative of a more widespread attitude in current social theory is that it puts science and technology at the centre of general social theory. What must be taken into consideration in Latour's studies is their centrality in current STS, which implicitly consider science and technology as the most important factors of modern society.

The Risk Society

According to Ulrich Beck, Anthony Giddens and Scott Lasch (1994) current reflexive modernisation or reflexive modernity is due to the success of modern ideals in the West, such as economic growth, universal suffrage and education, the welfare state, and civil and political rights. These changes mark a shift to the second modernity that is opposed to its earlier version, in the same way as the first modernity opposed feudal traditionalism. Therefore, the institutions of the first modernity are beginning to crumble in the face of economic and cultural globalisation. The state is starting to lose its importance with the rise of transnational forces (corporations, NGOs); the family is splitting apart with rising divorce rates due to the flexibility of work and women's liberation, thus losing its supportive function in the process; religion is reduced to a cultural artefact; and traditional political action is boycotted due to a lack of identification with the parties' goals. The old compromise between traditional institutions and the project of modernity building in industrial society is exceeded and individualisation as well as individual agency take centre stage. Nevertheless, late modernity is not a time of pure self-satisfaction. On the contrary, reflexive modernity calls into question modern fundamental assumptions by extending systematic doubt to the whole society (Beck, 1999). The global risk society as a result of reflexive modernisation is a hyper-technology-based society founded on the systematic relationship between production and science. On the one hand, technology and science are fundamental to producing wealth; on the other hand, however, a lot of unexpected consequences occur, affecting human health and the natural environment. In classical industrial society, a modernist view assumes realism in science, which creates a system in which scientists work in an exclusive and inaccessible realm – unexpected effects are banned. In the risk society, the authority of science is questioned but this critique, which is the basis of several social conflicts and movements, is often based on science; it is fundamental to highlight social risks as well as offering an alternative point of view on specific economic processes or public policies (Beck, 1986). In general, science and technology utilised by both big companies and conflictual actors, is part of a wider sub-politics. It is a decision-making system where decisions are based on a non-political method and it is made up of non-political actors (scientists, managers, experts, civil society, and so forth). Traditionally democratic political institutions, such as parliaments and political parties, react to the inputs from such a system rather than acting. In addition, sub-politics becomes more and more important, subtracting sovereignty from the State. In sum, according to Beck in late modernity, the ambivalence of science and technology is *structural* and is due to an emergent reflective effect of reflexive modernity: science and technology are both the problem and the solution within the risk society. That said, such an ambivalence is allocated just at the level of sub-politics whereas the official, democratic politics, is linearly connected to science and technology: the first is subordinated to the second. The civil society, including the techno-economic system as well as counter-power dynamics (Beck, 2006), takes priority over official democratic politics. However, is the ambivalence of the relationship between science and/ or technology and politics so limited? Furthermore, how is this relationship constructed overall concerning both its ambivalent and non-ambivalent aspects?

Reassembling the Social

The answer to these questions is at the centre of Latour's research. Similarly, to all theorists of complexity, such as Edgar Morin or Gregory Bateson, Bruno Latour (1991) takes leave of all unilateralistic forms of the critiques: *naturalisation, socialisation* and *deconstruction*. Within the first, *naturalisation*: subjects vanish to Nature; within the second, *socialisation*: science, technology and nature are replaced by human power; while in the third, *deconstruction*: everything becomes language and symbols. Each form cannot possibly combine with another. The result is a partial view of the world. By contrast, Latour argues that we need a social theory that develops a new kind of critique, as well as a new method capable of going beyond these limitations which are based on the constitution of modernity. According to Latour (2005), the traditional methodological discourse of social sciences has posited the existence of a specific sort of phenomenon called "society" or "social structure", meaning independent sets of variables to explain non-social phenomena, including individual behaviours. However, we would need to develop a new approach that considers social aggregates in order to explain: *focus should be on the different kinds of connections between heterogeneous things that are not in themselves social*, taking into consideration the relationship among different "operating principles" of such things. Agency is present in the world, although it is not individual but rather actor-network-based. The problem is to understand the *assembling dynamics* that establish these networks called "society". Within such a framework, Latour claims, that *We have never been modern* (1993), because, if, ever since the beginning, modern societies have produced, several hybrid networks defined by "imbroglios" or "mix" of politics, religion, law, fiction, technology, including human and non-human actors, the discourse of modernity has denied this reality. Ambivalence is the normal product of modernity in action, but simplification and separation (the obsession of order) are the main missions of a modern constitution. The main artificial separation is between "nature" and "culture" and, correspondingly, between "technoscience" (a category that Latour introduced in 1987) and "politics". According to the constitution of modernity, the representation of natural things in the laboratory is forever separated from the representation of humans by social contracts, public institutions and, in general, politics; a politics that is just for humans. Although recognising the hybridised reality created by modern society implies refuting the modern discourse based on institutional separation and conceptual depuration of fields, objects, phenomena and actors. Politics and technoscience are obviously connected in present-day society – without technoscience politics is an "empty container", lacking means and power; and, conversely, without politics, technoscience is irrelevant. In addition, confronting climate change: the nexus between society and technoscience, culture and nature, experts and political leaders, human and non-human actors, is the fundamental characteristic of our current politics (Latour, 2017). Thus, to recognise this ambivalence and re-think social and political institutions, which would enrich our democracy with new subjects and representative dynamics, is the greatest challenge of the present day (Latour, 2017).

Nonetheless, Bruno Latour's perspective underlines the close interconnection between technoscience and politics, going beyond the classical methodological alternative between individual agency and structuralism in a convincing way, and situating ambivalence at the level of such a connection – are we really sure that's all? On the contrary, should we not recognise that the nexus between politics and technoscience is producing a new kind of "structure" where ambivalence plays a strategic and specific role? We will confront these questions in the next parts.

Technocratic Politics: Politicisation of Science and Scientisation of Politics

Although Latour's and Beck's standpoints are very different in many respects, they seem to share two important conclusions: first, considering the relationship between politics and technoscience, ambivalence is always an emergent and unwanted consequence of social processes; and, second, ambivalence must be managed by actors, but it does not perform a specific role or function in a particular field created by the nexus between politics and technoscience as well as by their actors. Ambivalence is conceptualised as a sort of destiny in contemporary society, and is not considered a key theoretical matter: why are contradictory trends not recognised as "contradiction" by actors and observers? Why do contradictory trends produce ambivalence and not contradiction? Which kind of latent function can we recognise in this situation? Three simplistic answers are possible: because the Marxist paradigm has fallen into disgrace and contemporary scholars tend not to utilise its categories with a light heart. Secondly, the social world has changed and old categories (like contradiction) are unable to analyse it efficiently. Third, ambivalence exists; it is a fact, and the contemporary social world is chaotic by definition. So, we might conclude that the reason is in the observer's bias as well as in the structure of reality. Nevertheless, all these answers circumvent the problem: not considering the results of political or economic sociology concerning the relationship between technoscience and politics, not going beyond the disciplinary niche and such answers do not recognise that a new field has appeared: *technocratic politics*.

Technocratic Politics and Democracy

Technocratic politics is a politics based on various types of decision-making involving high-level bureaucrats, members of executive branches (e.g., ministries) and experts, seeking through the authority of technoscience both the content and legitimation of specific policies. Technocracy is not a specific political system or regime, but a relatively coherent set of structures and techniques (socio-technique system) based on the authority of expertise whose official function is to improve the efficiency and effectiveness of: 1) public decision-making, 2) implementation of policies and 3) ruling class recruitment and selection at various levels (Antonelli, 2019). The first and second aspects particularly concern Western countries, the third (under the name and ideology of "meritocratic system") is also an important element in countries such as the People's Republic of China, Singapore and Taiwan (Bell, 2015). In addition, technocracy is a means of constructing hegemony in society (Gramsci, 2011); its most important latent function. So, technocratic politics is a way of arranging different human (experts) and non-human actors (public statistics, artificial intelligence, computers, big data and so forth) that have come from outside traditional politics with other human (politicians, bureaucrats) and non-human (weapons, laws, public institutions and so forth) actors more typically found in the field of politics. Although the role of technoscience is important for social movement actors as well as in social conflicts (counter-power dynamics), for example, as Ulrich Beck (1986) or Alain Touraine (1978) have underlined in their research, technocratic politics concerns itself with the problem of governance *over* and within society.

One of the most prevalent misunderstandings is considering technocracy in opposition to politics: a widespread attitude initially supported by Habermas (1973) and other scholars such as Putnam (1977), Fischer (1990) and Esmark (2017). According to Habermas, the Second World War period saw a "new or second phase in the rationalization process" which Max Weber had already comprehended as the basis for bureaucratic domination, defined by the "scientization of politics". In this technocratic model, the relationship between the professional expert and the politician appears to have effectively "reversed itself", making the latter «a mere agent of a scientific intelligentsia, which, in concrete circumstances, elaborates the objective implications and requirements of available techniques and resources as well as optimal strategies and rules of control» (Habermas, 1971, p. 63). Starting from such a perspective the "thesis of depoliticization" began to prevail in technocracy studies. Esmark, quoting Putnam's research, sums up the essence of depoliticisation in six guiding principles:

1) The idea that the replacement of politics with technicians provides experts and professionals with an essentially apolitical role. 2) Scepticism and even hostility towards politicians and political institutions. 3) A more or less blatant disregard for the openness and equality of political democracy tending towards authoritarianism and absolutism. 4) The belief that social and political conflict is misguided or even contrived. 5) The interpretation of effective policy as a question of pragmatics, not ideology nor morality. 6) The notion that technological progress is good, and questions of social justice are unimportant.

(Esmark, 2017, p. 5)

Such a depoliticisation logic is also recognised by other researchers as a crucially dynamic inherent in the transformation from government to governance in a globalised era (Hay, 2007; Stoker, 2006).

However, all of these positions are not fully acceptable. Evidently, they seem to be based on a double misunderstanding: first, considering experts to be more powerful than they actually are; second, considering "politics" as a synonym of "democracy". Relative to Western societies, technocratic politics can surely be recognised as a means of reducing, limiting, or even eliminating the substantial role of representative institutions in public decision-making. Consequently, technocracy is not in opposition to politics on the whole, but it is in conflict with democratic politics, if democracy is defined as formal and representative as well as based on the centrality of mass political parties and their typical kinds of mediation and participation (Antonelli, 2019). The result is the formation of a post-democratic scenario (Crouch, 2000). In addition, as a category, technocratic politics allows us to go beyond the classic discourse on technocracy: starting from lucubration by Saint-Simon (2012) and Comte (1851-54) in the nineteenth century, passing to Veblen (1914; 1919), Scott (Segal, 2005) and Burnham (1941) in the first half of the twentieth century, Galbraith (1967), Bell (1973) and Khanna (2017) between the "Thirty Glorious Years" and global society, technocracy has been represented as the rise of a new subject based on more universal attitudes in governance than the "traditional" bourgeoisie or traditional political classes. However, even if technoscience has been systematically included in State and politics during all of those periods, it has never taken the place of the bourgeoisie and, above all, political leaders: as technocratic politics, technoscience and its actors have systematically helped to manage both society and social problems.

In this respect, it is no longer possible to consider ambivalence as a merely emergent effect produced by the nexus between technoscience and politics. Nor can the contradiction be seen as a residue of our past. Our thesis is that *ambivalence is a specific rule to assemble technocratic politics and its own contradictory trends in late modernity, with the function of avoiding the production of contradictions in the relationship between politics and society.*

Politicisation of Science, Scientisation of Politics

In general, the relationship between politics and technoscience is not technical but normative; the struggle is around what kind of norms and values prevail as a guide for decision-making. When technoscience is actually involved in politics, the "sphere of means" is not only in question as the classic Weberian perspective argues (Weber, 2004), but also, the "sphere of aims", because each "scientific" data, theory, suggestion, and advice as well an algorithm brings with it a specific vision of the world (Antonelli, 2019; Numerico, 2021). Particularly, if we consider social sciences: is contemporary economics detachable from its liberalist and individualistic premises? Is a market-based society just a more rational and efficient society in economics terms, or is it also thought of as a more ethical society? Foucault

(2004), as well as several other scholars interested in technological artefacts and politics (e.g., Winner, 1980) or data and politics (e.g., Supiot, 2017) have shown this absolute separation between "instrumental rationality" and "substantial rationality" to be misleading. So, technocratic politics is the field of a negotiation between actors from different worlds (politics and technoscience) concerning the *means and aims* of public policies as well as public agencies that must manage a particular set of them – as the quoted theory of de-politicisation argues (see above). The result is a doubly contradictory possibility in order to take into consideration a public issue: "politicisation of technoscience" and "scientization of politics" (Eyal, 2019). The first is a decision-making process in which technoscience standards are shaped to a political will; the second is a decision-making process in which technoscience standards prevail over political consideration. In the Covid pandemic crisis, the continuous changing of age groups to which the vaccine, Vaxzevria (formerly Covid-19 VaccineAstraZeneca), should be injected seems to be an example of the first kind of process, while the lockdown or stay-at-home policy is an example of the latter. Both are ambivalent processes: a political decision is also a scientific decision and *vice versa,* even if to varying degrees. At the *time of ideology*, in other words, during the twentieth century, all historical political ideologies, such as Fascism or Stalinism, incorporated some scientific elements or scientific presumptions: is Nazi racism and anti-Semitism thinkable without a reference to the biology of its time? Is it possible to imagine Stalinism without the claim of new social sciences to understand deep laws of history and society? Pseudoscience was the product of these embeddings, as Karl Bracher (1982) argues. So, ideological politics is used to subordinate science. Nowadays, the borderline between post-ideological and post-democratic politics, on the one side, and technoscience on the other, is intentionally unclear: "politicisation of politics" and "scientization of politics" are two possible mixes of norms and values, useful for claiming the production of more effective policies in a complex world; but, also, legitimation for public decisions in a reflexive modernity: in a volatile scenario, such as contemporary society, politics is weak and it needs to be mixed with technoscience. At the same time, such a mix does not have to be "peaceful" and "definitive" in its solutions or public representations. Instead, it must be open ended in order to maintain the possibility of an "exit-strategy" for political leaders.

Ambivalence, Expertise and Technocratic Politics

So far, we have talked about technoscience as an impersonal actor. However, it is impossible to understand the role of ambivalence in contemporary technocratic politics if we do not take into consideration the key function which supports the whole system: the expertise. The relationship between politics and technoscience is actually not based on a direct nexus between scientists and politicians. Such a relationship is mediated by a specific figure: the expert – an educated person who is embedded in the decision-making on the basis of their scientific reputation and status in a technical agency. In addition, sometimes such a person must share the same political orientation of the political leader who engaged them.

Several studies and typologies are focused on expert and expertise (e.g., Caselli, 2020; Robey and Marcus, 1984; Busso, 2011; Feldman and March, 1993; Weiss, 1979; Pielke, 2007; Osborne, 2004; Pellizzoni, 2003; 2011). Nonetheless, in our opinion the most important study in order to understand the role of ambivalence in technocratic politics is by Gil Eyal (2019). According to him, nowadays and, in particular, during the Covid pandemic crisis, while experts have never been more in demand they are now, also less credible than ever before. The two relations, dependence and distrust, feed off and amplify one another, generating an ambivalent situation. There are multiple processes and factors contributing to this dynamic:

1. *The intensification of jurisdictional struggles among experts*: in confronting a social problem, who is really an expert? What kind of expertise is necessary? Generally speaking, more answers are possible. So, turning to experts to imply conflicts of legitimation and visibility among different kinds of possible experts occurs (Abbott, 1988).
2. *The dynamic of "overflowing" of economic and technological risks*: the concept of overflowing introduced by Michel Callon in 1998, refers to the intrinsic difficulty an "expert" has in responding to a social problem because in late modern society technology changes very fast. Consequently, as Ulrich Beck (1986) argued, nobody is really an expert on a particular set of problems.
3. *The legitimation crisis of the capitalist state*: dealing with a complex society, in which many social claims from several different social groups, whose interests are contrasting, turn to politics, the legitimation of the state becomes increasingly weaker. Consequently, the state turns to other social external fields, experts and technoscience, but in doing so prolongs its legitimation crisis.
4. *The growth of regulatory science*: regulatory science is halfway between the fast time of law and politics, as decisions must be made quickly, and the long-time of science, necessary to argue and accurately test its hypotheses. Regulatory science, the domain of experts, connects the first to the second dimension, suggesting decisions that are not completely confirmed by science, lie in a context of uncertainty.

5. *The temporal dynamics of trust*: trust is always a lacking resource, particularly in the late modernity. So, experts must win the trust of politicians and citizens, but it is always "until further notice".
6. *The interplay between competing strategies for making the future present*: all advice by experts is a sentence like this: "if ... then". It is funded on scenarios and previsions that presume to make the "future present". The conflict among different kinds of experts around actualising alternative futures is one of the most pertinent of all.
7. *The collapse of academic and media gatekeepers*: the disintermediation of communication due to the rise and widespread use of digital technologies and the 2.0 web causes the crisis of prestige and authority of intellectuals and their respective institutions (e.g., university, newspapers, and so forth). Consequently, experts, who based our prestige on such institutions, have seen their authority diminish.
8. *The rise of lay expertise*: "lay expertise" is due to an increasing level of education among the population as well as greater social democratisation. Thus, "self-advocacy" is increasing, which means that people take positions against the pastoral power (Foucault, 2004) of experts and technoscience.

The analysis of Guy Eyal brings to light the core of our problem: the capacity to produce hegemony, legitimisation and decisions by democratic politics is increasingly reduced. Turning to technoscience is represented as a means of going beyond such limits. That said, when it is included in a political system, through expertise, it also becomes ever weaker as a political actor. What Eyal's analysis cannot see is technocratic politics: although fragile, the combination of technoscience and politics is not a limitation but rather a fundamental resource for power. Producing ambivalence, being founded on ambivalence, technocratic politics is able to play on ambiguity and execute public policies that would not be acceptable without the presence of expertise: in other words, ambivalence reduces the cost of accountability for political leaders and the ruling classes, thanks to actors who are not threatening to them. In this way both internal and external clashes that could lead to systematic contradictions are also avoided.

The Role of Ambivalence

There are two main conclusions in this chapter: the first, which is more specific, is that ambivalence at the crossroads between technoscience and politics is not just an emergent effect of unconnected processes, as Ulrich Beck argued. Rather, it is an operating principle of technocratic politics and a way of assembling heterogeneous elements with the latent function of managing ambiguity and complexity in the relationship between society and politics.

It enables a response to the chronic crisis of legitimation, effectiveness and efficiency of democratic politics, paradoxically using the weakness of technoscience in politics as a symbolic and political resource; a point undervalued by Bruno Latour.

Hypothetically, we can assume a more general second conclusion: in the contemporary world contradictory trends are incorporated within different sub-systems in order to expand the response capacity of structures. In modernity, if contradictory trends are thought of as a source of irrationality and de-stabilisation, in late modernity they can be considered and constructed as a source of stabilisation. Therefore, in general, ambivalence is the art of making contradictory trends co-exist, in order to use the resulting ambiguity as a resource, which is particularly useful for every social power to blend in and reduce the pressure of an omnipresent accountability. In this scenario, has contradiction disappeared? Should we agree with the mainstream opinion and talk just in terms of ambivalence, encountering contradictory trends within a specific social field? In both cases the answer is no. Logically and factually speaking, in late modernity, ambivalence is a cognitive and practical dispositive, widespread in society and in institutions precisely because the possibility of "contradiction", as a clash between opposite trends, is always an opportunity lying in wait. More precisely, ambivalence is reproduced in order to avoid contradiction; avoiding contradictory trends could produce instability in a world so complex as to be characterised by a deluge of them. Ultimately, we argue that, for social theory and social research, in a given situation, the challenge is to recognise when we are confronted with an "ambivalence" or a "contradiction" (releasing it from a specific philosophy of history) as well as their factual and logical relationships.

Note

1 A first version of this chapter has been published in *The Lab's Quarterly*, XXIII, 4, 2021 with the title of: *Avoiding Contradiction, Assembling Ambivalence. Social theory and technocratic politics.*

4   Emergency

The New Enlightened Despotism[1]

The purpose of this chapter is to analyse technocratic politics in the early phase of the Covid-19 crisis with a special focus on the "stay-at-home" phase in Italy. Any epidemic virus is not just a natural event. On the contrary, it should be considered a socio-political subject: in fact, being socially construed, it produces many socio-political effects resulting in social, economic, and political tensions and contradictions within a global system. For this reason, several scholars tend to speak more and more in terms of "syndemia" rather than "pandemia" facing phenomenon like the spread of the SARS-CoV-2 virus, which became universally known as Covid-19 (Horton, 2020; Singer *et al.*, 2017). Such a matter is particularly true concerning the fundamental link between politics and society. We are living in a new era which is radicalising both the impact and expert role of ICT (Information and Communications Technologies) in governance dynamics, a trend that had already started in a pre-pandemic world and is largely based on the centrality of government by emergency.

Technocratic Politics and Emergency

As we argued in the previous chapters, technocracy is not a specific political system or a regime but is a relatively coherent series of structures and techniques (socio-technique system) based on the authority of humans and not human expertise for improving the efficiency and effectiveness of: 1) public decision-making, 2) implementation of policies and 3) ruling class recruitment and selection at various levels (Antonelli, 2019). Public decision-making and implementation of policies particularly concern Western countries, and ruling class recruitment and selection at various levels, under the name and ideology of "meritocratic system", is also an important element in countries such as the People's Republic of China, Singapore or Taiwan (Bell, 2015). In addition, technocracy is a means for constructing hegemony in society (Gramsci, 2011), its most important latent function. Starting from

DOI: 10.4324/9781003217725-5

lucubration by Saint-Simon (2012) and Comte (1851-54), passing to Veblen (1914, 1919), Scott (Segal, 2005), Burnham (1941), Galbraith (1967), Bell (1973) and Khanna (2017), technocracy has been represented as the rise of a new social (and ruling) class, based on more universal attitudes in governance than the "traditional" bourgeoisie. As Alvin Gouldner (1979) argued, such a universal attitude should be based on:

> the culture of critical discourse (CCD) is an historically evolved set of rules, a grammar of discourse, which (1) is concerned to justify its assertions, but (2) whose mode of justification does not proceed by invoking authorities, and (3) prefers to elicit the voluntary consent of those addressed solely on the basis of arguments adduced. CCD is centred on a specific speech act: justification [...] The culture of critical discourse is characterized by speech that is relatively more situation free, more context or field "independent." This speech culture thus values expressly legislated meanings and devalues tacit, context limited meanings. Its ideal is: "one word, one meaning," for everyone and forever.
>
> (Gouldner, 1979, p. 45)

Despite these analyses, the matter is more ambivalent than it seems. On the one hand, both in industrial and post-industrial society, experts seem to have forged an alliance with different social classes and social élites, and they work to enforce the legitimation and effectivity of such classes to rule society: for example, if in "Thirty Glorious Years" (1950–1970) experts were allied with progressist and statist élites, nowadays globalisation is based on a serious of technocratic structures – in turn, fuelled by neo-liberalist values and cultures, such as the IMF (International Monetary Fund), World Bank and ECB (European Central Bank) at an international level or authorities and advisory committees at a national level – supporting the hegemony of global business élites to rule and to transform the world on the basis of their own interests and rationality – a product of the increasing interconnection between "substantive rationality" and "instrumental rationality" (see Chapter 1). On the other hand, hegemony produced by experts is not just ideological and political but also pragmatic: a technocratic-based hegemony works until it produces more effective solutions for public problem-solving; its crisis starts when such solutions stop being effective and new social problems arise. Thus, during "Thirty Glorious Years" experts and politicians have held a bias towards myopic unsustainable policies, which have led to severe macroeconomic shocks since the 1960s. The solution to monetary instability and stagflation was the "independence of central banks", implemented since the 1980s. The change in policy was successful in counteracting inflation, which initially enhanced the credibility of neo-liberal technocrats. However, the recent financial crisis has diminished this credibility: it is in such a moment that reproduction of old fashioned, scientific-based solutions, at first promoted on a "culture of critical discourse", degrade into ideology. New experts, new scientific-based solutions and, probably, new socio-political élites are called for in response to these new conditions.

These trends point out the meaning relationship between "technocracy" and "emergency" and, more generally, between "expertise" and "emergency". As Guy Eyal argues: "the expert is typically called upon to speak not about what she routinely does and knows best, but about a new problem, only one aspect of which is germane to her area of expertise" (Eyal, 2021: 24). So, as Niklas Luhmann says: "an expert is a specialist to whom one can put questions that he is unable to answer". The typical style of their discourses is *promissory*: based on their experience and their knowledge (regulatory science), they are called by politics to aim to explore and to give advice in a field and relative to a set of problems that nobody knows in depth – experts included – full of uncertainty and ambiguity. "Emergency" is the typical condition where all this manifests itself. For this reason, in an ever-changing society, an emergency is the order of the day, and it is the main field where experts act. As we have argued in the chapter three, ambivalence is the typical style for technocratic politics and, generally speaking, for politics, to manage this situation, playing it in their favour. At the same time, all of this reveals the strong relationship between "emergency", "expertise" and "sovereignty" in current societies. The studies by Giorgio Agamben (2005) can help us to understand this fundamental point. Starting from Carl Schmitt's theory, Agamben notes that political life is subject as much to the contingent and the unpredictable as it is to any normality anticipated by the law. The contingent and the unpredictable form the basis of the state of exception. The sovereign must first decide when a state of exception exists and, second, decide upon which strategies – including the suspension of normal legal processes – to deal with it. These include, above all, calling a state of emergency. There is thus a correlation between the sovereign and the exception. The exception has no power as such (for the exception is determined by the sovereign); however, without the exception, it would be impossible for the sovereignty to exist and to maintain itself. Following this argument, we can say the expert in the emergency is similar to the *homo sacer* (Agamben, 1998) – it is inside the system and, in particular, the juridical system—because without a juridical act, it cannot legitimately take action—and, at the same time, it is outside the system, because it must force the ordinary social life. All of this tells us that technocracy is not the contrary to the politics but a particular form of it in a contemporary world.

60   *Emergency*

As we have already argued in the first and in the third chapters, one of the most prevalent misunderstandings is considering technocracy in opposition to politics: a widespread attitude initially supported by Habermas (1971) and other scholars such as Putnam (1977), Fischer (1990) and Esmark (2017). According to Habermas, the Second World War period saw a "new or second phase in the rationalization process" which Max Weber had already comprehended as the basis for bureaucratic domination, defined by the "scientization of politics". In this technocratic model, the relationship between the professional expert and the politician appears to have effectively "reversed itself", making the latter «a mere agent of a scientific intelligentsia, which, in concrete circumstances, elaborates the objective implications and requirements of available techniques and resources as well as optimal strategies and rules of control» (Habermas, 1971, p. 63). Starting from such a perspective the "thesis of depoliticization" began to prevail in technocracy studies. Esmark—quoting Putnam's research—sums up the essence of depoliticisation in six guiding principles:

1) The idea that the replacement of politics with technicians provides experts and professionals with an essentially apolitical role. 2) Scepticism and even hostility towards politicians and political institutions. 3) A more or less blatant disregard for the openness and equality of political democracy tending towards authoritarianism and absolutism. 4) The belief that social and political conflict is misguided or even contrived. 5) The interpretation of effective policy as a question of pragmatics, not ideology nor morality. 6) The notion that technological progress is good, and questions of social justice are unimportant.

(Esmark, 2017, p. 5)

Such a depoliticisation logic is also recognised by other researchers as a crucially dynamic inherent in the transformation from the government to governance, in a globalised era (Hay, 2007; Stoker, 2006).

Nevertheless, not all these positions are not fully acceptable. Evidently, they seem to be based on a double misunderstanding: first, considering experts more powerful than they actually are; second, considering "politics" as a synonym of "democracy". Relative to Western societies, technocratic politics can be surely recognised as a means for reducing, limiting or even eliminating the substantial role of representative institutions in public decision-making. Consequently, technocracy is not in opposition to politics on the whole but it conflicts with democratic politics, especially if democracy is defined as formal and representative as well as based on the centrality of mass political parties and their typical kinds of mediation and participation

(Antonelli, 2019). On the same basis, technocratic politics can be seen as the opposite to neo-populism. As a "political style" (Diamanti and Lazar, 2018), neo-populism is based on a set of values completely different to technocracy: argumentative simplification, the myth of popular absolute sovereignty, emotional communication and voluntarism. Therefore, if neo-populist politics is only based on "ethics of conviction", technocratic politics aspire to be also founded on "ethics of responsibility", in a Weberian sense (Weber, 2004). And this is the order of discourse with which it presents itself to the public.

Covid-19 Pandemic Crisis between Expertise, System Tensions and Public Opinion

The first step of our analysis is to recognise the nature of the crisis: it is a global health emergency. In such a case, the crisis is socially and politically constructed in relation to a natural event, although many analysts point out that the spread of Sars-Covid19 and its spill-over from a bat to mankind is due to human irresponsibility.[2] If this is the case, we are dealing with three fundamental elements: first, science (the biology and medicine) is essential to define the threat and how to manage it. Second, since the virus is new, the medicine proceeds through "trials and errors", based on a series of subsequent systematic studies, through comparison with past pandemic dynamics, clinical practice as well as the effects of new vaccination campaigns. Thus, the medicine is in a learning process characterised by uncertainty, differing opinions, and heated discussions among experts. This situation seems to anticipate a typical risk to society scenario (Beck, 1986): on the one hand, everyone depends on scientific authority and, probably, definitive answers are expected by experts, due to the strength of the science myth; on the other hand, the normal uncertainty of scientific debate, accentuated currently, comes to light. Thus, public opinion may be disoriented; an effect probably amplified by the dynamics of contemporary global communication, characterised by a systematic information overload, media over-exposure of experts and the multiplication of echo-chambers on social media. As Edgar Morin argues:

> Ce qui me frappe, c'est qu'une grande partie du public considérait la science comme le répertoire des vérités absolues, des affirmations irréfutables [...] Très rapidement, on s'est rendu compte que ces scientifiques défendaient des points de vue très différents, parfois contradictoires [...] Toutes ces controverses introduisent le doute dans l'esprit des citoyens

Translation to English:

> What strikes me is that a large part of the public considered science as the repertoire of absolute truths, irrefutable affirmations […] Very quickly, we realized that these scientists were defending points of view very different, sometimes contradictory […] All these controversies introduced doubt into the minds of citizens
>
> (Morin, 2020 cit. in Ghezzi, 2020).

As a consequence, a partial immaturity of Western democracy not to fully include the typical dynamics of a "technical democracy" seems to come to light. In fact, according to Michel Callon, Pierre Lascoumes and Yannick Barthe (2011) rapid scientific and technological advances create uncertainty and bring about unforeseen concerns – a condition that is also evident in the Covid-19 virus. Thus, while the formation of "hybrid forums" (in which experts, non-experts, ordinary citizens, and politicians come together) are revealing the limits of traditional delegative democracies, there is a failure to include this practice in public decision-making (deliberative democracy) as well as public opinion and experts not joining such conversations in a constructive way.

> Concerning Italy at least, in the first phases of the pandemic crisis, it has been possible to partially test these arguments utilising the findings of "Science in Society Monitor" by Massimiliano Bucchi and Barbara Saracino who have conducted a survey on this topic, in a representative sample of Italians, carried out on 6 April 2020.[3] Thus, we can deduce that «Almost half of all Italian citizens think that the range of advice publicly given by experts has created confusion.»
>
> (Bucchi and Saracino, 2020).

Thirdly, within the whole articulation of the pandemic crisis, we can hypothesise the presence of a double cultural and systemic tension due to the characteristics of modernity – particularly second modernity (Beck, 2000). The first tension is between the promise of the modern society to guarantee a condition of well-being for everybody, particularly in health-care – for example in the World Health Organization's (WHO) Constitution. We can read that its main objective is «the attainment by all peoples of the highest possible level of health» (chapter 1, art.1) – and political, technical and economic opportunities to respect such a promise.

At a subjective level, this means that people expect a high standard of protection by society and government, on the basis of a sort of "total security and zero risk" myth (Bauman, 2006; Battistelli, 2016); an expectation depending on the characteristics of the political system (included citizens' rights) as well as cultural background but, at any rate, present in every modern society, even if not democratic – for example, as Bell (2015) argues in the People's Republic of China, the capacity of the party and the government to protect its people is a fundamental expectation of all. When a crisis or emergency with the characteristic of a "black swan" arises, such expectations dramatically increase, producing a tremendous overload on institutions (Taleb, 2007): clearly this has occurred in the case of the Covid-19 pandemic crisis.

At a systemic level, correspondingly, the capacity to respond to this overload is based on available technical, organisational and economic resources, given the means of production and the need to protect them. Thus, such a situation produces a legitimisation, stability and governmental crisis that, according to Luhmann's social system theory, pushes the system to attempt a complexity reduction in order to save itself (Luhmann, 1984): the national "stay-at-home strategy"[4] adopted by governments in dealing with the spread of Covid-19 in Spring 2020 could be seen as an application of that operation, as it does not just impose isolation and quarantine, but also the blocking of non-essential economic and social activities, in order to preserve the health of the population as well as the healthcare system itself. A first-time social experiment and measure that, surprisingly if we consider the normal behaviours of society and, in particular, those of democratic "open societies" based on the cult of Liberty (Bauman, 2000), have had a good support across all worldwide public opinion in the first phase of the emergency: according to the "Global Behaviours and Perceptions in the Covid-19 Pandemic" survey, conducted by Thiemo Fetzer and his research team in 58 countries and with over 100,000 respondents between late March and early April 2020:

> most respondents reacted strongly to the crisis: they report engaging in social distancing and hygiene behaviors, and believe that strong policy measures, such as shop closures and curfews, are necessary. They also believe that their government and their country's citizens are not doing enough and underestimate the degree to which others in their country support strong behavioural and policy responses to the pandemic
> (Fetzer *et al.*, 2020, p. 1).

In addition, such a survey highlights that even the mental health of people seems to improve when the government introduces stronger measures of social distancing and control (Fetzer *et al.*, 2020).

A second kind of systematic tension is between such a safety need and the hyper-speed of the global socio-economic system, a fundamental imperative necessary for achieving increasing degrees of development. Thus, if the need for safety and protection requests the prevalence of medical and public order understanding and measures, the need for hyper-speed leads to balancing those with economic and sociological knowledge in order to preserve, in a long-term perspective, the reproduction system; including the availability of economic resources to support both public health measures and combat the increase of poverty, social marginality and unemployment linked to a massive reduction of social and economic complexity.

On the basis of the "nature" of the that crisis, the observation seems to suggest that the development of a particular *technocratic politics* could be seen as a fundamental way to manage the crisis and, in particular, to manage the analysed systemic tensions within.

Changing Political Configuration: Technocratic Politics at the Beginning of the Covid-19 Crisis

As the Covid-19 pandemic crisis is a worldwide health emergency, it requires medical knowledge in order for it to be defined as well as managed. While the virus has been spreading worldwide the power of medical experts has grown everywhere: without medical expertise a policy against the virus (including lockdown) would be unthinkable; and could not be justified to citizens. However, this is only partially true: at the beginning of the crisis, the power of medical experts has actually been increasing as a consequence of the government's increasing role in controlling the economy and society; producing a radical deviance (a sort of "cognitive dissonance") from the *vulgate* of neo-liberalism but confirming the strong relationship between expertise and emergency. In other words, politics integrates experts and not the contrary. Thus, a question arises: *when and how have medical experts and medical expert structures been included within the new technocratic politics at the time of the Covid-19 crisis?* Despite regional and national variations, it is possible to identify a general pattern in answering such a question while more detailed studies identify cross-national differences.

Relative to the "when", starting from China to the USA, passing from Italy to the UK, everywhere signs of the spread of Covid-19 and their consequences are, in the first phase, systematically undervalued. Just ahead of the early severe effects, in terms of death and congestion of healthcare systems, governments started to react by involving medical experts and medical expert structures in decision-making. At the top level, starting with the World Health Organization (WHO), such structures have just had an advisory role: in a world more and more interconnected but still dominated by national sovereignty, "suggesting" and "monitoring", rather than deciding, have been their main responsibilities. Different from structures like the ECB, they are weak technocratic institutions, depending on politics and its discretionary power. Nevertheless, their role has been fundamental in pushing governments towards stronger containment measures, including "stay-at-home" strategies and, at the same time, justifying them to the public on behalf of the science community. Such action was a clear response to the first systematic tension (between the promise of the modern society to guarantee a condition of well-being for everybody and the political, technical and economic opportunities to respect such a promise) which we have already discussed: reducing socio-economic complexity in order to preserve both a functioning system and citizens' health. At this point, in any case, it is important not to overvalue the "wisdom" of medical experts in comparison to the "lightness" of political authorities in the early phases of the pandemic crisis: in fact, one of the most important factors that explain the delays in adopting measures, such as the "stay-at-home" instruction, in order to contain the epidemic, is in the weakness of the scientific community concerning this new phenomenon. According to Pietro Ghezzi (2020), beginning in the 1980s, health policies are determined on an evidence-based medical approach (EBM): every decision must be made based on scientific evidence and reliable data. Unfortunately, here this was not the case: SARS CoV-2 was unknown, and all relevant data about it was very incomplete. Therefore, this makes for weakness in medical experts' dealings with political authorities. The consequence is that both experts and ruling classes have learned the best responses step-by-step, resulting in a "lockdown" solution, recommended by WHO and based on previous epidemic crises rather than scientific evidence connected with Covid-19. Nevertheless, following the declaration of lockdown, such technocratic politics based on a strong dialogue between governments and experts with a progressive marginalisation of parliaments (post-democracy situation), a massive expansion of public intervention towards society and the economy and the limitation of some fundamental rights (in particular the freedom of movement); these seem to have established a particular political configuration (polity) next to the traditional "enlightened despotism" or "Police State" based on technocracy.

Within our framework, "enlightened despotism/police state" is not a simple synonym of "absolute state" or "authoritarian state" even if centralised political authoritarianism is one of the most important characteristics of this socio-political configuration. Looking at it as a whole, such an expression refers to the original sense of practices and theory on police function, which is strongly linked to the rise of the Modern State between the seventeenth and eighteenth centuries, a phenomenon well-analysed by Michel Foucault (2004a; 2004b). In such a context, the "Police" is not just a public activity against crime (security) but a complex government activity based on the premise of achieving public well-being as a basic reason for the existence of the Sovereignty, even if an authoritarian sovereignty seeks more power. As early as 1531, Thomas Elyot wrote an important book titled *The Book named the Governor,* where the ruler was compared to a medical doctor of the political body: "Police" is the name of this commitment towards the more general public and civic health. As Giuseppe Campesi argues «this kind of state had to take care of everything [...] a right of interference that went further than the need to guarantee the survival of subjects, until taking charge of the whole material and moral social life» (Campesi, 2009, p. 126). According to the *Traité de la police* (1717) by Nicolas De La Mare «the police may be described in eleven matters: religion; way of life; discipline; public health; liberal arts and sciences; foods; public order and security; trade; manufactories; domestic servants; workers» (De La Mare, 1717, p. 4). If we consider the whole complex of socio-political effects emerging due to the lockdown situation and, in general, the way of managing the struggle against the virus, it is possible to identify some similarities between the traditional police state and current political configuration; particularly the relationship between the state and its citizens:

1. The re-organisation of the whole state activity towards the aim of protecting citizens and to directly assure their well-being
2. The need to regulate every aspect of social life, including social, and informal relationships
3. The reduction of many civil rights, particularly the right of freedom of movement
4. The need for discipline and self-discipline as well as a more cogent informal social control to implement the rule of law as well as to protect public and individual health
5. A massive use of law enforcement agencies to control citizens' behaviour.

Obviously, relative to Western countries, there are also more differences:

1. A post-democratic situation rather than an authoritarian one
2. The official transitional nature of the current configuration
3. The conservation of several civil rights as "habeas corpus" and the freedom of expression.

For such reasons we must speak in terms of a "grey" situation rather than a full technocratic police state. In addition, we must underline that the use of digital technology and the role of experts – also beyond the role of medical experts – is a really interesting aspect within such a configuration:

1. Similarly, to every contemporary state and society strongly influenced by a technocratic system (for example Taiwan or Singapore) the grey technocratic configuration has been also an info-State, based on digital technologies in order to function (Khanna, 2017; Antonelli, 2019). A national "stay-at-home" strategy itself as well as contact tracing for preventing virus diffusion has been possible thanks to digital technologies and, in general, ICT: they have enabled the remote continuation of many public and private activities (e.g., smart working or school and university lessons), communicate in a more effective way, control virus expansion as well as citizen behaviour and so on. The famous Marx sentence seems particularly appropriate: «mankind thus inevitably sets itself only such tasks as it is able to solve». An observation that includes a pandemic like this: for example, in the 1980s it would have been less likely as the speed of socio-economic contact was much slower than nowadays. On the other hand, if the SARS-CoV-2 virus had spread in that time, without digital technologies, it would have been a greater catastrophe as a national "stay-at-home" strategy would have been unthinkable, given the technological limitations of that era
2. The dependence on data, data gathering and data processing to manage the situation in real time and take decisions
3. The roles of experts and expert knowledge in managing and defining the situation, including the legitimisation (or de-legitimisation) of decision-making as well as improving state efficiency. A factor that is leading governments – such as the Italian government – to involve new social science experts in crisis management, particularly for arranging the imminent post-lockdown phase and confronting the second systemic tension previously analysed and the tension between safety and the hyper-speed of the global socio-economic system
4. The dependence on scientists as well as pharmaceutical companies to develop a cure and an effective vaccine against the virus in order to end the crisis
5. The dependence on global and regional technocratic structures (e.g., ECB) to guarantee all possible help with both the medical and economic effects of the crisis; including the development of closer international cooperation among different national states; a mission that does not eliminate the emerging political economy of the pandemic and its geo-political effects, but rather includes them in a particular frame, more disciplined – the European Union, for example.

Beyond the Emergency

Although our analysis is only an immediate, impressionist, and interpretative one based on incomplete data and a variety of journalistic sources, it provides some relevant indications to enrich the theory of technocratic phenomenon. Technocracy seems to introduce a principle of rationality in governance which allows the tackling of systematic tensions exacerbated by the spread of Covid-19, and thus legitimising public decisions. It has provided a general framework for the latter initially based on the culture of critical discourse (Gouldner, 1979), establishing standard objectives as well as a rational means to achieving them. Nevertheless, technocracy is an indispensable means for managing the crisis and is clearly subordinated to the ruling class: in particular, the government determines "when" and "how" to utilise technocracy and not the contrary. In other words, technocracy is a way to enforce governability, in full continuity with a pre-pandemic world. At the same time, techno-science supporting the emergency is based on the extensive use of digital technologies, radicalising both the virtualisation of society and enforcing "digital platform capitalism" (Vecchi, 2017).

Both government and the public trust experts and techno-science in order to reduce uncertainty, to cope with threats and to manage personal and systemic stresses. For the first time in recent years, on a mass level, technocratic mechanisms have become a more public affair. Expectations are very high. However, techno-science has gradually revealed its internal divisions and conflicts and public opinion has become more and more disoriented. In other words, the Covid-19 crisis, since its beginning, has revealed immaturity between experts and the public in communicating with each other. Such a fact tends to reduce the capability of technocratic mechanisms in legitimising public choice as well as reducing the influence of neo-populist discourse in the long term.

How have political configurations (polity) changed? Our hypothesis is that a grey technocratic configuration next to the classic enlightened despotism/police state has characterised the "stay-at-home" strategy. Probably, constituting a model of crisis management for the future. This standpoint, linked to what has been argued about the incommunicability between public opinion and experts, underlines the need to reintroduce scientific debate, concerning the social uses of techno-science, to a democratic environment. Contributing to change the authoritarian use of scientific knowledge in relation to politics, as technocratic mechanisms, can actually lead to social empowerment; a challenge particularly important in a post-pandemic world.

Notes

1 A first version of this chapter has been published in *Rivista Trimestrale di Scienza dell'Amministrazione*, 2, 2020 with the title of: "Emerging Aspects in Technocratic Politics at the Time of the SARS COVID19 Crisis"

2 It seems that mankind has heavily contributed to Covid-19 spill-over and its incredible world-wide diffusion in a very short time in two ways: 1. By an excessive promiscuity among different animal species caught for commercial reasons. 2. Through the high speed of human mobility due to globalisation dynamics. For an analysis of both aspects see in particular: "'Tip of the iceberg': is our destruction of nature responsible for Covid-19?" The Guardian, 18th March 2020, available at: https://www.theguardian.com/environment /2020/mar/18/tip-of-the-iceberg-is-our-destruction-of-nature-responsible-for -covid-19-aoe.

3 As we can read on the influential "World Mapper" website: «Since 31 December 2019, when WHO was informed about the first cases in Wuhan, China, more than 2.5 million people are confirmed to have contracted Covid-19 (Coronavirus) from the SARS-CoV-2 virus and more than 175,000 have died (all figures last updated 23 April, 2020). There are now cases of Covid-19 on all continents, in 215 countries/territories. The highest mortality rates are found in the British Virgin Islands with 25% (one death in 4 cases), followed by Nicaragua (20%), France (18.1%), Saint Martin (15.5%) and Belgium (14.9%). Twenty-one countries have a mortality of 10% or higher. Of the larger countries with reported cases in the thousands, France has the highest reported mortality rate (18.1%) followed by Belgium (14.9%), the United Kingdom (13.6%), Italy (13.4%), Sweden (12.1%) and the Netherlands (11.6%). After correcting the number of deaths in Wuhan, China now has a mortality rate of 5.5% (up from 4%), only slightly higher than the United States (5%). Of the countries with many reported cases, Germany, Turkey and South Korea have a considerably lower mortality rate of 3.4%, 2.4%, and 2.2% respectively) » (https://worldmapper.org/maps/ coronavirus-cases-mortality/). The problem is that the mortality rate is calculated on the formula: deaths\cases. Unfortunately, if different countries tend to record causes of death in different ways, the greatest bias in such statistics is the estimation of cases: as many studies argue (for example the report-13 "Estimating the number of infections and the impact of non-pharmaceutical interventions on Covid-19 in 11 European countries" by Imperial College MRC Centre for Global Infectious Disease Analysis) the number of Covid-19 cases is heavily underestimated in all countries. Thus, the real Covid-19 mortality rate should be much lower than it appears in official statistics and, on the contrary, morbidity rate much higher than it seems.

4 A "lockdown" order (Europe) or a "stay-at-home" order (North America) or a "movement control order" (Southeast Asia) is an order from a government authority to restrict movements of a population as a mass quarantine strategy for suppressing, or mitigating, an epidemic or pandemic, by ordering residents to stay at home except for essential tasks or to work in essential businesses. In many cases, outdoor activities are allowed. Nonessential businesses are either closed or adapted to working from home. It is based on WHO "Country & Technical Guidance - Coronavirus disease (Covid-19)" available at: https://www.who.int/ emergencies/diseases/novel-coronavirus-2019/technical-guidance.

Bibliography

Abbott A. (1988). *The System of Professions*. Chicago: Chicago University Press.

Adorno T., & Horkheimer M. (2010). *Dialectic of Enlightenment*. Stanford: Stanford University Press [first edition 1947].

Adorno T.W., Albert H., Dahrendorf R., Habermas J., Pilot H., & Popper K.R. (1981). *Positivist Dispute in German Sociology*. London: Heinemann Educational Books.

Agamben G. (1998). *Homo Sacer Sovereign Power and Bare Life*. Redwood City: Stanford University Press.

Agamben G. (2005). *State of Exception*. Chicago: Chicago University Press.

Airoldi M., & Gambetta D. (2018). "Sul mito della neutralità algoritmica", in *LQ: The Labs Quarterly*, *20*, 4.

Anselmi M. (2018). *Populism: An Introduction*. London: Routledge.

Antonelli F. (2007). *Caos e postmodernità. Un'analisi a partire dalla sociologia di Michel Maffesoli*. Roma: Philos.

Antonelli F. (2008). "Da rivoluzionari a dirigenti. Movimenti, élites ed innovazioni nella seconda modernità", in *Mutamenti della politica nell'Italia contemporanea*, *I*. Edits by Segatori Roberto, Barbieri Giovanni. Soveria-Mannelli: Rubbettino. pp. 183–200.

Antonelli F. (2019). *Tecnocrazia e democrazia. L'egemonia al tempo della società digitale*. Roma: L'Asino d'Oro.

Bacon F. (2009). *The New Atlantis*. open access edition [first edition 1627].

Bakunin M. (1980). "On the International Workingmen's Association and Karl Marx", Bakunin on Anarchy, translated and edited by Sam Dolgoff, 1971. Retrieved on February 24th, 2009 from www.marxists.org. Proofread online source RevoltLib. com, retrieved on July 15, 2020.

Balbi P., & Magaudda C. (2014). *Storia dei media digitali. Rivoluzioni e continuità*. Roma-Bari: Laterza.

Balbi P., & Magaudda C. (2018). *Fallimenti digitali. Un'archeologia dei «nuovi» media*. Milano: Unicopli.

Bauman Z. (1989). *Modernity and the Holocaust*. Ithaca: Cornell University Press.

Bauman Z. (1991a). *Legislators and Interpreters: On Modernity, Post-Modernity and Intellectuals*. London: Polity.

Bauman Z. (1991b). *Modernity and Ambivalence*. Ithaca. Cornell University Press.

Bauman Z. (1997). *Postmodernity and Its Discontents*. London: Polity Press.

Bauman Z. (2000). *Liquid Modernity*. Cambridge: Polity Press.

Bauman Z. (2006). *Liquid Fear*. Hoboken: Wiley & Sons.

Battistelli F. (2016). *La sicurezza e la sua ombra*. Roma: Donzelli.

Beck U. (1986). *Risikogesellschaft*. Frankfurt am Main: Suhrkamp.

Beck U. (1999). *World Risk Society*. Cambridge: Polity.

Beck U. (2000). *The Brave New World of Work*. Cambridge: Cambridge University Press.

Beck U. (2006). *Power in the Global Age*. Malden: Polity Press.

Beck U., Giddens A., & Scott L. (eds.) (1994). *Reflexive Modernization. Politics, Tradition and Aesthetics in the Modern Social Order*. Cambridge: Polity.

Bell A.D. (2015). *The China Model: Political Meritocracy and the Limits of Democracy*. Princeton: Princeton University Press.

Bell D. (1973). *The Coming of Post-Industrial Society: A Venture in Social Forecasting*. New York: Basic Books.

Beniger R.J. (1986). *The Control Revolution. Technological and Economic Origins of the Information Society*. Harvard: Harvard University Press.

Bloor D. (1991). *Knowledge and Social Imagery*. Chicago: University of Chicago Press.

Bourdieu P. (1984). *Homo Academicus*. Paris: Editions de Minuit.

Bracher D.K. (1982). *Zeit der Ideologien: Eine Geschichte politischen Denkens im 20*. Stuttgart: Verlags-Anstalt GmbH.

Braudel F. (1988). *La dinamica del capitalismo*. Bologna: il Mulino [first edition 1985].

Bucchi M., & Saracino B. (2020). "Italian citizens and covid-19: One month later – April 2020', in *Science in Society Monitor*. Available at: https://sagepus.blogspot .com/2020/04/italian-citizens-and-covid-19-one-month.html.

Burnham J. (1941). *The Managerial Revolution: What is Happening in the World*. New York: John Day Co.

Busso S. (2011). *L'informazione nelle politiche sociali. Modelli teorici, processi di legittimazione e dinamiche organizzative*. Roma: Carocci.

Callon M. (1998). "An essay on framing and overflowing: Economic externalities revisited by sociology", in *The Sociological Review*, *46*(1_suppl), 244–269.

Callon M., Lascoumes P., & Barthe Y. (2011). *Acting in an Uncertain World: An Essay on Technical Democracy*. Boston: MIT Press.

Campesi G. (2009). *Genealogia della pubblica sicurezza. Teoria e storia del moderno dispositivo poliziesco*. Verona: Ombre Corte.

Campo D., Martella E., & Ciccarese S. (2018). "Gli algoritmi come costruzione sociale. Neutralità, potere e opacità", in *LQ: The Labs Quarterly*, *20*(4), 10.

Caselli D. (2020). *Esperti. Chi sono e come studiarli*. Bologna: il Mulino.

Chen L., Hannak R., & Wilson C. (2018) "Investigating the impact of gender on rank in resume search engines", in Proceedings of the 2018 Chi Conference on Human Factors in Computing Systems, *651*, 1–14.

Comte A. (1851–54). *Système de politique positive ou Traité de sociologie instituant la religion de l'Humanité*. Paris: Carilian-Gœury et V. Dalmont.

Crouch C. (2000). *Post-democracy*. Cambridge: Polity Press.

Dargent E. (2014). *Democracy and Technocracy in Latin America. The Experts Running Government.* Cambridge and New York: Cambridge University Press.

De La Mare N. (1717). *Traité de la police, Où l'on trouvera l'histoire de son établissement, les fonctions et les prérogatives de ses magistrats ; toutes les loix et tous les réglemens qui la concernent : On y a joint une description historique et topographique de Paris, & huit Plans gravez, qui representent son ancien Etat, & ses divers accroissemens, avec un recueil de tous les statuts et réglemens des six corps des marchands, & de toutes les Communautez des Arts & Métiers....* 2 vol. in-folio, J. et P. Cot: Paris. 1705–1710. Available at: https://gallica.bnf.fr/ark:/12148/bpt6k1098988.image.

Desrosières A. (1993). *The Politics of Large Numbers. A History of Statistical Reasoning.* Harvard: Harvard University Press.

Diamanti I., & Lazar M. (2018). *Popolocrazia.* Roma-Bari: Laterza.

Di Felice M. (2017). *Net attivismo.* Formigine: Edizioni Estemporanee.

Dolgoff S. (ed.) (1980). *Bakunin on Anarchism.* Montreal: Black Rose Books [first edition 1872].

Dostoyevsky F. (2003). *The Brothers Karamazov.* London: Penguin [first edition 1880].

Esmark A. (2017). "The technocratic take-over of democracy: connectivity, reflexivity and accountability", Paper prepared for ICPP 2017, Singapore T07P08: The Accountability and Legitimacy of Knowledge Experts in Policy Making.

Eyal G. (2019). *The Crisis of Expertise.* Cambridge: Polity.

Feldman M.S. and March J.G. (1993). "L'informazione delle organizzazioni come segnale e simbolo", in March J.G. (a cura di), *Decisioni e organizzazioni.*Bologna: il Mulino.

Fetzer T., Witte M., Hensel L., Jachimowicz, J., Haushofer, J., Ivchenko, A., … Yoeli, E. (2020). "Global behaviors and perceptions in the COVID-19 pandemic", PsyArXiv. April 16. https://doi.org/10.31234/osf.io/3kfmh. Available at: https://psyarxiv.com/3kfmh.

Feurbach L. (2012). *The Essence of Christianity,* Digireads.com [first edition 1841].

Fischer F. (1990). *Technocracy and the Politics of Expertise.* Newbury Park/London/New Delhi: Sage.

Flinders M., & Bullerb J. (2006). "Depoliticisation: Principles, tactics and tools", in *British Politics, 2006*(1), 293–318.

Florida R. (2003). *The Rise of the Creative Class: And How It's Transforming Work, Leisure, Community and Everyday Life.* New York: Basic Books.

Formenti C. (2000). *Incantati dalla rete. Immaginari, utopie e conflitti nell'era di Internet.* Milano: Raffaele Cortina.

Formenti C. (2008). *Cyber-soviet. Utopie post-democratiche e nuovi media.* Milano: Raffaele Cortina.

Foucault M. (2003). *Sécurité, Territoire, Population. Cours au Collège de France (1977–1978).* Paris: Galimard.

Foucault M. (2004). *Naissance de la biopolitique. Cours au Collège de France (1978–1979).* Paris: Galimard.

Foucault M. (2008). *Les Mots et les Choses. Une archéologie des sciences humaines.* Paris: Galimard [first edition 1967].

Foucualt M. (2020). *L'Histoire de la sexualité*. Paris: Galimard [first edition 1976].

Freud S. (2021). *Civilization and Its Discontents*. New York: W W Norton & Co Inc [first edition 1930].

Fukuyama F. (1992). *The End of History and the Last Man*. New York: Free Press.

Galbraith J.K. (1967). *The New Industrial State*. Boston: Houghton Mifflin Harcourt.

Galeotti M. (2018). "Discriminazione e algoritmi. Incontri e scontri tra diverse idee di fairness", in *LQ: The Labs Quarterly*, *20*, 4.

Garin E. (1988). *L'uomo del Rinascimento*. Roma-Bari: Laterza.

Ghezzi P. (2020). "Vivere nell'incertezza', in *il Mulino. Rivista di cultura e di politica*, 21 April. Retrieved from: https://www.rivistailmulino.it/news/newsitem /index/Item/News:NEWS_ITEM:5183 (21/04/2020).

Giddens A. (1991). *The Consequences of Modernity*. London: Polity Press.

Gillespie T. (2016). "Algorithm", in B. Peters (ed.), *Digital Keywords*. Princeton: Princeton University Press.

Gouldner A. (1970). *The Coming Crisis of Western Sociology*. New York: Basic Books.

Gouldner A. (1979). *The Future of Intellectuals and the Rise of the New Class: A Frame of Reference, Theses, Conjectures, Arguments, and an Historical Perspective on the Role of Intellectuals and Intelligentsia in the International Class Contest of the Modern Era*. London: Palgrave.

Gramsci A. (2011). *Prison Notebooks*: Cambridge, MA: Harvard University Press.

Green M.C., Strange J.J., Brock T.C. (Eds.) (2002). *Narrative Impact: Social and Cognitive Foundations*. London: Psychology Press.

Habermas J. (1971). *Toward a Rational Society*. London: Heinemann.

Habermas J. (1973). *Legitimationsprobleme im Spätkapitalismus*. Frankfurt am Main: Suhrkamp.

Hall S. (1986). "Gramsci's relevance for the study of race and ethnicity", in *Journal of Communication Inquiry*, *10*(2), 5–27.

Harvey D. (1973). *Social Justice and the City*. Athens: University of Georgia Press.

Hay C. (2007). *Why We Hate Politics*. Cambridge: Polity.

Hayek F. (1980). *The Counter-Revolution of Science: Studies on the Abuse of Reason*. New York: Liberty Fund Inc. [first edition 1952].

Hobsbawm E.J. (1995). *The Age of Extremes: The Short Twentieth Century, 1914– 1991*. London: Micheal Joseph.

Horkheimer M. (2000). *Eclipse of Reason*. New York: New Publisher [first edition 1947].

Horton R. (2020). "Offline: COVID-19 is not a pandemic', in *The Lancet*, *396*, 874. https://doi.org/10.1016/S0140-6736(20)32000-6.

Jasanoff S., & Kim S.H. (eds.) (2015). *Dreamscapes of Modernity. Sociotechnical Immaginaries and the Fabrication of Power*. Chicago: University of Chicago Press.

Joly P.B. (2010). "On the economics of techno-scientific promises", in M. Akrich, Y. Barthe, F. Muniesa, & P. Mustar (eds.), *Débordements. Mélanges offerts à Michel Callon*. Paris: Presses des Mines.

Kant I. (2012). *Beantwortung der Frage: Was ist Aufklärung?* Scotts Valley, California: CreateSpace Independent Publishing Platform [first edition 1784].

Katz H. (2017). *Manufacturing an Artificial Intelligence Revolution: Neoliberalism and the 'new' big data Yarden Katz*. Harvard: Harvard University.

Keuth H. (2015). "The positivist dispute in German sociology: A scientific or a political controversy?", in *Journal of Classical Sociology*, *15*(2), 154–169.

Keynes J.M. (1936). *The General Theory of Employment, Interest and Money*. London: Macmillan.

Khanna P. (2017). *Technocracy in America: Rise of the Info-State*. Scotts Valley, California: CreateSpace Independent Publishing Platform.

Kojève A. (1980). *Introduction to the Reading of Hegel: Lectures on the Phenomenology of Spirit*. Ithaca: Cornell University Press.

Kuhn T. (2012). *The Structure of Scientific Revolutions*. Chicago: University of Chicago Press [first edition 1962].

Lasch C. (1996). *The Revolt of the Elites: And the Betrayal of Democracy*. New York: W. W. Norton & Company.

Latour B. (1987). *Science in Action. How to Follow Scientists and Engineers Through Society*. Cambridge, MA: Harvard University Press.

Latour B. (1991). *We Have Never Been Modern*. Cambridge, MA: Harvard University Press.

Latour B. (2005). *Reassembling the Social: An Introduction to Actor-Network-Theory*. Oxford: Oxford University Press.

Latour B. (2017). *Ou atterrir? Comment s'orienter en politique*. Paris: La Decouverte.

Luhmann N. (1984). *Soziale Systeme. Grundriß einer allgemeinen Theorie.* Frankfurt am Main: Suhrkamp.

Luhmann N. (2012). *Macht im System*. Berlin: Suhrkamp [first edition 1969].

Lyotard J.F. (1979). *The Postmodern Condition: A Report on Knowledge*. Minneapolis: University Of Minnesota Press.

Maffesoli M. (2003). *Notes sur la postmodernité: Le lieu fait lien*. Paris: Editions du Félin.

Magatti M. (2009). *Libertà immaginaria. Le illusioni del capitalismo tecno-nichilista*. Milano: Feltrinelli.

Magatti M. (2018). *Oltre l'infinito: Storia della potenza dal sacro alla tecnica*. Milano: Feltrinelli.

Manin B. (2017). *Principi del governo rappresentativo*. Bologna: il Mulino [first edition 1995].

Marcuse H. (1974). *Eros and Civilization: A Philosophical Inquiry into Freud*. Boston: Beacon Press [first edition 1955].

Marcuse H. (1991). *One-Dimensional Man: Studies in the Ideology of Advanced Industrial Society*. Boston: Beacon Press [first edition 1964].

Marx K. (2018). *The Capital*. New York: Penguin.

Marx K., & Engels F. (2014). *The Comunist Manifesto*. Mumbai: Sanage Publishing House.

Merton R.K. (1968). *Social Theory and Social Structure*. New York: Free Press [first edition 1949].

Merton R.K. (1976). *Sociological Ambivalence and Other Essays*. New York: Free Press.

Merton R.K. & Barber E. (1963). "Sociological ambivalence", in Tiryakian E.A. (ed.), *Sociological Theory, Values and Sociocultural Change: Essays in Honor of Pitirim A. Sorokin*. London: Free Press of Glencoe.

Mosco V. (2004). *The Digital Sublime: Myth, Power, and Cyberspace*. Cambridge, MA: MIT Press.

Mounk Y. (2018). *The People vs. Democracy: Why Our Freedom Is in Danger and How to Save It*. Cambridge: Harvard University Press.

Netkin R. (2018). *The Chinese Social-Credit System Experience: A National Reputation System in the Making*. Moutain View: Amazon Books.

Noble S.U. (2018). *Algorithms of Oppression: How Search Engines Reinforce Racism*. New York: New York University Press.

Numerico T. (2021). *Big data e algoritmi. Prospettive critiche*. Roma: Carocci.

O'Neil C. (2016). *Weapons of Math Destruction. How Big Data Increases Inequality and Threatens Democracy*. Danvers: Crown Publishing Group.

Ortega y Gasset J. (1999). *La rebelión de las masas*. Madrid: Espansa [first edition 1930].

Osborne T. (2004). "On mediators. Intellectuals and the ideas trade in the knowledge society", in *Economic and Society*, *33*(4), 430–447.

Pellizzoni L. (2003). "Knowledge, uncertainty and the transformation of the public sphere", in *European Journal of Social Theory*, *6*(3), 327–355.

Pellizzoni L. (2011). *Conflitti ambientali. Esperti, politica, istituzioni nelle controversie ecologiche*. Bologna: il Mulino.

Pielke R.A. (2007). *The Honest Broker. Making Sense of Knowledge in Policy and Politics*. Cambridge: Cambridge University Press.

Platone (2007). *La Repubblica*. Roma-Bari: Laterza.

Popper K.R. (1945). *The Open Society and Its Enemy*. London: Routledge.

Putnam R. (1977). "elite transformation in advanced industrial societies: An empirical assessment of the theory of technocracy", in *Comparative Political Studies*, *10*(3), 383.

Ridley F.F. (1966). "French technocracy and comparative government", in *Political Studies*, *14*(1), 34–52.

Robey D., & Marcus M.L. (1984). "Rituals in information system design", in *MIS Quarterly*, *1*, 5–15.

Rousseau J.J. (2004). *The Social Contract*. New York: Penguin [first edition 1762].

Saint-Simon H. (2012). *Œuvres completes*. Paris: PUF.

Sartre J. P. (1960). *Critique de la raison dialectique*. Paris: Gallimard.

Sartre J.P. (1996). *L'existentialisme est un humanisme*. Paris: FOLIO ESSAIS [first edition 1945].

Schluchter W. (2004). "Introduzione", in M. Weber, *La scienza come professione. La politica come professione (1919)*. Torino: Einaudi.

Schwab A. (1917). "Beruf und Jugend", in *Die weißen Blätter*, *4*(5), 97–113.

Segal H.P. (2005). *Technological Utopianism in American Culture*. New York: Syracuse University Press.

Segatori R., & Barbieri G. (2008). *Mutamenti della politica nell'Italia contemporanea*. Soveria-Mannelli: Rubbettino.

Simon H.A. (1947). *Administrative Behavior: A Study of Decision-Making Processes in Administrative Organization*. New York: Macmillan.

Singer M., Bulled N., Ostrach B., & Mendenhall E. (2017). "Syndemics and the biosocial conception of health', in *The Lancet*, *389*, 941. https://doi.org/10.1016 /S0140-6736(17)30003-X.

Smelser N.J. (1998). "The rational and the ambivalent in the social sciences", in *American Sociological Review*, *63*, 1–16.

Stoker G. (2006). "Public Value Management: A New Narrative for Networked Governance?", in *The American Review of Public Administration*, *36*(1), 41.

Streek W. (2013). *Gekaufte Zeit: Die vertagte Krise des demokratischen Kapitalismus*. Frankfurt am Main: Suhrkamp Verlag.

Supiot A. (2017). *Governance by Numbers, The Making of a Legal Model of Allegiance. Hart Studies in Comparative Public Law*. London: Bloomsbury Publishing.

Taleb N.N. (2007). *The Black Swan: The Impact of the Highly Improbable*. New York: Penguin Random House.

Tilly C. (1978). *From Mobilization to Revolution*. Reading: Addison-Wesley.

Touraine A. (1978). *La voix et le regard (Sociologie permanente)*. Paris: Seuil.

Touraine A. (2013). *La fin des Société*. Parisi: PUF.

Touraine A. (2018). *Défense de la modernité*. Paris: Ed. du Seuil.

Vacca G. (2017). *Modernità alternative. Il Novecento di Antonio Gramsci*. Torino: Einaudi.

Veblen T. (1914). *The Instinct of Workmanship and the State of the Industrial Arts*. New York: MacMillan.

Veblen T. (1919). *The Place of Science in Modern Civilisation and Other Essays*. New York: B.W.

Vecchi B. (2017). *Il capitalismo delle piattaforme*. Roma: Manifestolibri.

Wallerstein I. (2004). *World-Systems Analysis: An Introduction*. Durham: Duke University Press Books.

Weber M. (2004). *Wissenschaft als Beruf. Politik als Beruf*. Tübigen: Mohr Siebek Ek. [first edition 1919].

Weber M. (2019). *Economy and Society: A New Translation*. Cambridge: Harvard University Press.

Weich K.E. (1995). *Sensemaking in Organizations*. London: Sage.

Weigert A.J. (1991). *Mixed Emotions: Certain Steps toward Understanding Ambivalence*. Albany, NY: State University of New York Press.

Weiss C.H. (1979). "The many meanings of research utilization", in *Public Administration Review*, *20*, 462–431.

Westerlund G. (1979). *Organizational Myths*. New York: Harper & Row.

Winner L. (1980). "Do artifacts have politics?", in *Dedalus*, *109*(1), 121–136.

Ziman J. (2000). *Real Science: What it is, and What it Means*. Cambridge and New York: Cambridge University Press.

Index

For Product Safety Concerns and Information please contact our EU
representative GPSR@taylorandfrancis.com
Taylor & Francis Verlag GmbH, Kaufingerstraße 24, 80331 München, Germany

* 9 7 8 1 0 3 2 1 0 9 2 6 8 *